Number 11 Autumn 2005

Editor: Jon Cook
Deputy Editor: Katri Skala
Assistant Editor: Sarah Gooderson
General Manager: Sarah Gooderson
Design & Production: Julian p Jackson
Editorial Assistants: Megan Bradbury & Joe Dunthorne

Pretext Editorial Board: Jon Cook (Chair), Christopher Bigsby, Patricia Duncker, Richard Holmes, Ian McEwan, Michèle Roberts, Vic Sage, Val Striker, Val Taylor.

Founding Editors: Julia Bell & Paul Magrs

Thanks to the following for making this magazine possible: Arts Council England, the School of Literature and Creative Writing and the Centre for Creative and Performing Arts at the University of East Anglia.

SUBMISSIONS: *Pretext* is published twice a year. We do not acknowledge receipt of submissions and, due to the volume of material, it may take up to five months to hear back from us. If you wish to have your work returned, please enclose an SAE. For more detailed submission guidelines, please turn to pages 144-145.

TO SUBSCRIBE: call 01603 592783 or e-mail info@penandinc.co.uk. One year's subscription for individuals (two issues) costs £14 (UK), £16 (Europe), £18 (rest of world); for institutions £18 (UK), £20 (Europe) £22 (rest of world). Or visit our website <http://www.inpressbooks.co.uk/penandinc>.

Introduction: © Jon Cook, 2005
Selection: © The Editors, 2005
Contents: © The Individual Authors, 2005
Cover design & photos: © Jeremy Webb / Pen & Inc Press

All rights reserved. No part of this publication may be reproduced or transmitted, in any form or by any means, electronic or mechanical, including photocopying, recording or any information storage or retrieval system without prior permission.

Pretext is published by Pen & Inc Press, School of Literature and Creative Writing, University of East Anglia, Norwich, Norfolk NR4 7TJ and distributed by Central Books, 99 Wallace Rd, London, E9 5LN.

Pretext/Pen & Inc Press is a member of Inpress Ltd. – Independent Press Management.

ISBN: 1-902913-23-x

Printed and bound by Antony Rowe Ltd, Bumper's Farm, Chippenham, Wiltshire SN14 6LH.

Contents

Introduction
Jon Cook   v

Five Poems
Seamus Heaney   1

Blind Date
Luisa Valenzuela   7

The Difference of View
**Patricia Duncker
& Michèle Roberts**   15

Kindness
Ron Butlin   31

Four Poems
David Solway   39

Honey, I Shrunk The Planet
Richard Beard   45

The Silk Road Chandlery
Errol Scott   51

An Interview with Iain Sinclair
Sebastian Groes   65

The Gilded Man
plus Four Poems
Alison Croggon   81

A Family Affair
Michael Holroyd   95

This Breathing World
José Luis de Juan   99

Writing A Tale
Sarah Gooderson   107

Welcome!
Dubravka Ugresic   121

Boilers
Cecilia Rossi   129

Biographical Notes   137

Jon Cook
Introduction

In an essay first published in 1942 the American poet, Wallace Stevens, gave a sonorous statement about the nature of a poet's work. It was, he claimed, 'a violence from within that protects us from a violence without. It is the imagination pressing back against the pressure of reality.' For Stevens this force in poetry was connected to a thought about nobility, but not to a definition of it. He wanted to break free from the belief that nobility is something connected to a discredited past. Instead it was a capacity to experience 'our spiritual height and depth'. As the phrasing of his argument makes clear, Stevens was thoroughly alert to the likelihood that he would be misunderstood. He did not think of himself as defending a conservative ideal, but he knew that to use a term like 'nobility' was to be immediately placed in an ideological minefield.

Like a number of the pieces published in this issue of *Pretext*, Stevens's essay raises a question about the polemical character of literature. Does strong and lasting work arise from a sense of opposition and anger? And what if the 'pressure of reality' includes forms of literature to be overcome or contested? The exchange of emails between Michèle Roberts and Patricia Duncker begins in a polemic against what they see as the dismal character of recent 'women's interest fiction'. Patricia Duncker invokes a return to the 'Utopian rage' that gave an earlier generation of women writers their linguistic energy and imaginative boldness. Iain Sinclair, in his interview with Sebastian Groes, claims that 'UEA's creative writing department is responsible for producing some of the most horrendous writers around today'. It's a well-worn theme

Introduction

and one which Sinclair pauses to consider as he recalls the work of W. G. Sebald. But Sinclair, like Michèle Roberts and Patricia Dunker, is angered by a loss of radical spirit and independent creation associated with the 1960s. In her essay, Dubravka Ugresic speculates on the future of literature in a world of multinational corporations and projects for European unification. She's not entirely pessimistic, but the polemical edge remains strong. To celebrate the difference and diversity of writers from smaller European countries does not necessarily result in them reaching a wider audience. Or if they do, it will be based on a narrow selection of authors.

Pretext 11, like previous issues of the magazine, is committed to sustaining a debate about what people read – or don't read – and why. Outspoken argument is one way of resisting that 'pressure of reality' that can easily lead to the stifling conformities of taste or fashion. But the imagination's 'pressing back' does not need to take the form of an overt polemic. It can be felt in apparently quiet and meditative form: in Seamus Heaney's remarkable sequence of poems about schooling, for example, published here for the first time. These poems do not simply retell the past. They illuminate it and in ways that show how a childhood world develops its own reality amidst the signs of political violence. Something similar happens in Cecilia Rossi's story *Boilers*. Errol Scott's *The Silk Road Chandlery* places an imaginary world in the midst of a real one and creates some strange and exhilarating transfigurations.

In the last issue of *Pretext* we reported briefly on the first event organized by The New Writing Partnership, a unique collaboration between Norwich City Council, Norfolk County Council, Arts Council England, East, and the University of East Anglia. In June this year, the Partnership organized its second event, New Writing Worlds. Writers came from many different parts of the world to Norwich and UEA for ten days of workshops and debate. Some readers may have read a report of the event in a recent issue of the *Times Literary Supplement*. We are delighted to publish the work of some of the writers who contributed to New Writing Worlds: Alison Croggon, David Solway, Ron Butlin, and Dubravka Ugresic.

Jon Cook

'Internationalism' is an uneasy word. Applied to literature it can assume that writers are securely placed in a national context from which they speak or write to other nations. *Pretext* is a magazine committed to publishing international writing, but that must mean something more than just publishing work that comes from a lot of different countries. The travelling or exiled imagination has been vital to modern literature. As discussion at the New Writing Worlds event made clear, the nation – its myths and its demands – can be part of that 'pressure of reality' that the strong imagination must resist. The 'spiritual height and depth' that Stevens wrote about may include a national identity, but it is not just a national identity. What we hope this issue of *Pretext* offers is work that shows how the horizons of the familiar world can be shifted by the presence of a new imaginative fact or idea. It is in moments like this that an imaginative world takes shape. The cartography of these imaginative worlds may well bear the imprint of political nations. But there is also a sense of moving elsewhere, either beyond the nation or to a place within it that is no longer national.

Seamus Heaney
Five Poems

THE PLAYGROUND
After René Char

The blows that flattened him hurled him at the same time far ahead. He saw how it would be in years to come, how he'd still be there, bleeding on the ground, but with this difference: whereas now he faced the malignity of one in particular, in future it would be general, a constant in his life.

Ever after, he would worm himself back down there, into that knowledge, its innocence and dumbness, like a bush being suckled by its roots, a smashed bush holding up inside its struck down branches.

What happened at the time was flight, escape, a flooding joy. He got away to the meadow, to a screen of reeds where he crouched to knead the mud and stare long at the trembling, desiccated fringes. The noblest, most enduring things earth had brought forth had adopted him, it seemed, to make amends.

And so again and again he would pick himself up and never once turn tail, fit to stand his ground and hold his own, that much more vulnerable and that much stronger.

René Char, 'L'Adolescent Soufffleté', from *Les Matinaux* (1950).

Senior Infants:

1. The Sally Rod

On the main street of Granard I met Duffy
Whom I had known before the age of reason
In short trousers in the Senior Infants' room
Where once upon a winter's day Miss Walls
Lost her head and cut the legs off us
For dirty talk we didn't think she'd hear.
'Well, for Jesus' sake,' cried Duffy, coming at me
With his stick in the air and two wide open arms,
'For Jesus' sake! D'you mind the sally rod?'

Seamus Heaney

2. A Chow

I'm staring at the freshly scratched initials
Of Robert Donnelly in the sandstone coping
Of Anahorish Bridge, with Robert Donnelly
Beside me, also staring at them.
                                  'Here,' he says,
'Have a chow of this stuff,' stripping a dulse-thin film
Off the unwrapped ounce of Warhorse Plug –
Bog-bank brown, embossed, forbidden man-fruit
He's just been sent to buy for his father, Jock.

The roof of my mouth is thatch set fire to
At the burning-out of a neighbour, I want to lick
Bran from a bucket, grit off the coping stone.
'You have to spit,' says Robert, 'a chow's no good
Unless you spit like hell,' his ginger calf's lick
Like a scorch of flame, his quid-spurt fulgent.

3. One Christmas Day in the Morning

Tommy Evans must be sixty now as well. The last time I saw him was at the height of the Troubles, in Phil McKeever's pub in Castledawson, the first time we'd met since Anahorish School. I felt as free as a bird, a Catholic at large in Tommy's airspace.

Yet something small prevailed. My father balked at a word like 'Catholic' being used in company. Phil asked if we were OK. Tommy's crowd fenced him with 'What are you having, Tommy?'

I was blabbing on about guns, how they weren't a Catholic thing, how the sight of the one in his house had always scared me, how our very toys at Christmas proved my point – when his eye upon me narrowed.

I remembered his air-gun broken over his forearm, my envy of the polished hardwood stock, him thumbing the pellets into their aperture. The snick of the thing then as he clipped it shut and danced with his eye on the sights through a quick-quick angle of ninety degrees and back, then drilled the pair of us left-right to the back of the house.

The Evanses' chicken coop was the shape of a sentry-box, walls and gable of weathered tongue-and-groove, the roofing-felt plied tight and tacked to the eaves. And there above the little neat-hinged door, balanced on the very tip of the apex, was Tommy's target: the chrome lid of the bell of his father's bike. Whose little zings fairly brought me to my senses.

Seamus Heaney

THE NOD

Saturday evenings we would stand in line
In Loudan's butcher shop. Red beef, white string,
Brown paper ripped straight off for parcelling
Along the counter edge. Rib roast and shin
Plonked down, wrapped up, and bow-tied neat and clean
But seeping blood. Like dead weight in a sling,
Heavier far than I had been expecting
While my father shelled out for it, coin by coin.

Saturday evenings too the local B-Men,
Unbuttoned but on duty, thronged the town,
Neighbours with guns, parading up and down,
Some nodding at my father almost past him
As if deliberately they'd aimed and missed him
Or couldn't seem to place him, not just then.

Luisa Valenzuela
Blind Date
Translated by Maxine Swann & Pola Oloixárac
An extract from the novel The Journey

She didn't question her acts, that Friday noon while leaving an elegant black briefcase in the cloakroom of the Museum of Modern Art in New York City. As an anthropologist, she was trained to study other people's behaviors, but not her own. It was a small briefcase, almost a male purse, luxurious and full and of the best make and best leather, for in this sort of exchange you can't be petty and everything must have style. Nor did she feel at any moment the temptation to open the briefcase and peek at its contents. She could get a pretty good picture, anyway, since she had let herself be tempted to collaborate in writing the letter of instructions.

The Saturday before, not having anything better to do, she had gone with Ava Taurel, famous dominatrix at your service, through the streets of Greenwich Village looking for a loup. Ava had taken her by surprise by calling and inviting her to a party. Let's get together this afternoon and have a good chat, we hardly know each other, Ava had said to her on the phone. So they got together, and just after saying hello Ava informed her point blank that they had to go out and look for some kind of sexy loup to cover her face because a very formal prospective client had contacted her on the phone and he shouldn't be allowed to see her at the party, in case he was at the party, and that's why I need a mask, Ava added.

The man can't be too formal if he's about to be Ava's client, she thought. All the same she liked the idea of going around the Village looking for a loup on that sunny afternoon, so far from any carnival or Halloween that there were no masks to be found.

Blind Date

They did find other useful gear for Ava's trade that Ava bought randomly in stores, things like six inch high red stiletto heels with long straps to wrap your calves in beautiful symmetrical bars. Symmetry, Ava explained to her patiently, is most respected in this business, a whole art consisting of constrictions.

And she, a humble observer, could only ask herself what the fuck was she doing there while Ava went on describing in detail how the prospective client shouldn't recognize her because he expected a perfect blind date; unilateral blindness, Ava made it clear, 'cause I know enough about the guy as to concoct a trap he'll fall into happy and hurting, as it should be.

The party was to take place that very Saturday night. Ava explained she had invited her to wise her up a bit, 'cause you might seem sophisticated but inside you're a candid anthropologist who doesn't know much about the actual facts of life. That's why it was crucial to change her appearance, Ava insisted, and as they drifted in search of the elusive loup they decided to look for the right outfit for her. It had to be suggestive, so that it wouldn't be out of place at such a special event. She resisted many of Ava's suggestions until she finally found, in a vintage store, a languid black satin dress with an open back.

Happy with the dress, she let herself be guided along Eighth Street as far as Broadway, where they began to pick through the clothes in the street stalls. In the fourth or fifth one Ava got excited about some bustiers in embroidered leather, full of promise, and decided to buy one. In the middle of the sidewalk Ava took off her blouse, tried the bustier on and her enormous tits overflowed giving her the triumphal air of someone who knows she's majestic, not grotesque. Some passersby lingered to applaud, someone said It looks fabulous on you, buy the gold one, don't get the black one. This was pure Greenwich Village, and Ava laughed. Watch out, she warned Ava, your formal client might be one of these chaps around here walking his dog.

Impossible, Ava knew well. The formal man, as could be inferred from his voice, wore a suit and tie and carried a minuscule cell phone, only walked in Central Park, lived just by the MoMA where he surely worked, a curator or an executive of some sort, and he wouldn't have a dog. He surely led a very conventional life, in no way associated with the blind date he had himself ordered by resorting not to a Miss Lonelyhearts, as would have been logical, but a Miss Lonelyasses of unforeseeable consequences.

And this was the mission of this woman who had named herself Ava Taurel and called herself her friend in spite of being only an acquaintance among acquaintances, whom she was accompanying beyond Lower Broadway, disguising her discomfort.

You have to come up with a good story for me, Ava told her along the way; not that I lack imagination, of course, I'm one of the very best in a business that requires subtle imagination and lots of chutzpah, but my new very formal client demands a perfect blind date, something totally new and unknown, and I know my own gig too well, what can I say, Ava went on, singing her own praises, walking along the streets aimlessly, having given up entirely looking for a mask

Ava went on and on, in English of course, asking for a good script for the plot. She, for her part, could only think about approaching the man in question, a man who was perhaps decent as well as formal – though these are all illusions, as always, she said to herself – to try to save him, even though she knew that no one has the right to save others from their own ghosts.

Ava's blind date would be a leap into the abyss, a disappearance. And at the end of the walk she began to infer that her task was limited to watching, to looking from all angles as far as possible, trying not to lose sight of a single detail.

What's all this about hiding your face? she finally said to Ava.

Let him be the blind one, blindfold him, hood him, 'block him out', as the torturers used to say in my long lost Argentina.

Good idea though not original at all, sighed Ava.

She shrugged her shoulders. A thousand years ago in the ethnography classes, she had learned not to get involved in changing the behavior of the species under observation. Forget it, she told Ava.

Ava was not one to abandon her prey, though, and finally convinced her with the bait of the MoMA as the site of the action. Together they set up the plot.

Blind Date

And at twelve noon the following Friday, according to the pre-established plan, she left the briefcase-handbag in the museum cloakroom, put the receipt in the addressed envelope Ava had given her for that purpose, and headed to the counter to buy a ticket even though nobody was watching her. Then, like a visitor who wants to consult a catalogue or something, she turned towards the museum's library. She leafed through some books, inspected the postcards on the rack, and a little while later was out on the street. She then went to the adjacent building's lobby to give the doorman the envelope containing the receipt from the cloakroom. It's an urgent message, she said to him. Possibly in the interest of self-defence she avoided taking note of the recipient's name or the number of his apartment.

The first stage of the plan completed, she would have been able to go on with her daily life until the appointed time, but she felt she shouldn't lose momentum or break her concentration or, even worse, get bored. She decided to go back to the museum and eat lunch quietly in the cafeteria in front of the sculpture garden and afterwards, with perfect calm, go look at the exhibition space between the front door and the cafeteria, nothing more than that, where her countryman Kuitca was showing mattresses covered with maps of ominous cities made for sleep travel along nightmare streets, mattresses somewhat burnt or singed, with cigarette marks, mattresses on the brink of death, like the ones Ava frequented could sometimes be. Or as later could become the mattress in the building next door, belonging to the blind date man who would become blind in his turn. A mattress that would get smeared with sperm – as he would hope – maybe with blood, piss, sweat or tears; the indelible mark of bodily fluids, scorched maybe, boiling. So she imagined.

On the main floor of the MoMA, the big rooms were taken up by the work of Kurt Schwitters. She spent the rest of her waiting time there. With a careful eye she followed the labyrinths made of the superimposed clippings, she studied the construction, the texture, the composition of each collage. There were many of them and she tried to tell herself a story in front of each one, and saw the reflection of her own life, also made of clippings, of superimposed threads and scraps of paper, of fragmented, blurred and alien faces.

Luisa Valenzuela

I'm alone in this museum, in New York, in the world; I'm alone and I have a Schwitters-like life, with barely the cohesiveness of these clippings, she thought.

She had come here to shape a blind date that didn't involve her at all, that was not about to give her satisfaction of any sort nor a remedy for solitude. Patience. It was just a matter of waiting for a while, gathering courage for later, just a little bit, just enough to deliver her speech without even looking at the face of the man in question, and most of all avoiding that he see her. A minimalist blind date inside the other one, the real one, merely putting it together, orchestrating it. She'd rather stay here with Schwitters; she didn't feel the urge to go to the top floor where the museum's collection was displayed in all its splendour.

Upstairs, the scenario of an unthinkable encounter awaited her.

Who stopped her from running away? Who obliged her to confront him? Had she signed a contract? Were they watching her? Nothing like that. She had gotten into this mess of her own will, and very much of her will she could have escaped in the very same instant to her house and gotten on with her life.

Wouldn't that be the most sadistic of all things, to leave the man waiting for a blind date that would be so blind it would turnout to be inexistent?

Sister, she said to herself, already a bit detached, as if on another level of consciousness, a level where anything can happen, where it's best to let things play themselves out; sister, you accepted and not only accepted but put your two cents into setting up this plot, you have to follow it through, no last minute ducking, no hypocrisy, that's not behavior worthy of you, sister, my little nun, sweet sister Charity now hooked up in this good deed for the benefit of tortuous desire.

What a bore, Schwitters, obsessive, repetitive, if I pull a thread I'm naked in front of this clinical eye that tortures paper into a thousand bits and then sews them back together with disconcertingly harmonious stitches.

If I pull... And yes, I pull.

The crazy impulse to tear off glued papers to see what hid behind them tore her – precisely – away from her thoughts and

Blind Date

not without a certain horror she realized it was time. The much feared, Lorcian five o'clock in the afternoon. She ran towards the entrance to plant herself in front of the gards, she had to lookout for a man with a discreet, elegant briefcase hanging from a shoulder strap. She decided to wait at the bottom of the escalator, a very conspicuous place but this didn't bother her, she could be just another visitor to the museum with a somewhat intellectual look. She pretended to read a brochure, peeking beyond it at pocketbook level. And all of a sudden she spotted him, recognized the briefcase, the same one she had left in the cloakroom that very morning.

The man was quite young, and to top it off dressed in a range of beige. Classy. She would have liked him for a romp in the hay, but not with his dark inclinations and the black briefcase, no.

He headed to the men's room with a careless step; she could foresee his movements as if she were watching him. He'll lock himself in the stall, sit on the toilet seat and, being a meticulous man, he'd put down the lid, unless he has something else or some physiological business besides following the instructions in the letter to take care of. He's astonished and then smiles to himself and maybe even wets his lips when finding the net stockings, the adjustable garter belt, the bra and matching black lace panties. He takes off his pants. He takes off his underwear and puts them in the briefcase, as if to get them out of his sight, and, naked, returns to sit on the toilet lid and goes on reading the instructions. She could follow him with her mind, she knew the letter by heart because she had helped write it, even though she hadn't come up with the idea (she knew little of these matters, preferred to know little, though she accepted and accepts that she'd like to know substantially less little than is advisable). The letter tells the man how to get dressed under his conservative pants and shirt. The letter directs him to take a seat in the middle of the central bench of the Pollock room, with his back to the entrance door. And cross your legs tight, it orders, to reveal the stockings that will be the signal to the person who will sit right behind you and give you the final instructions. And don't turn your head, don't look behind: remember Lot's wife, remember Orpheus, all those unremitting souls.

Luisa Valenzuela

Black lace net stockings, with a flowery pattern, very retro. She didn't need to pass in front of the man to see what he was exhibiting so provocatively: female stockings, a far cry from good taste, from manhood, from his pale brown suede sport shoes. She recognized the suit, the briefcase, it was him there seated in the middle of that long, wide bench. She let him study the Pollock drippings in front of him until he went cross-eyed. Go try to find a message there, she thought, it's always good to sound works of art looking for messages. It's always good and useless, that's the beauty of it.

The choice seemed on target to her, and not only because of the spacious bench. Suddenly she remembered that in London Jackson Pollock was called Jack the Dripper, the pun made sense in this case, it was to be hoped that the man sitting there had made the same association. She sensed he was smiling, she didn't need to walk in front of him to see it, a smile a little excessive, satisfied, not sure of itself but enjoying the suspense.

She took a deep breath and sat down behind the man, using him almost as a backrest so he couldn't turn around. He shivered and she took courage: Remember the Gorgon – she whispered – not only looking back hurts, sometimes also what is seen hurts.

Shit, she thought, I'm already off my script, adding unnecessary words to my speech. But she sensed a slight shiver in the other's stiff back and that ratified (gratified?) her.

She put her head in the hollow under the nape of the man's neck; she was far shorter than he was, but at that moment she felt a lot taller because she was giving the orders. Toss your head back a little if you hear me well, she whispered, and he obeyed and it was as if he had tried to caress her. I'm not your blind date, she said to the man; I'm just the spokesperson transmitting the orders. You go home now, take a sharp razor and cut the briefcase open, carefully because it has a false bottom, and what you find there you'll put on your head, covering your face well and closing all the zippers to block your orifices. But before you do that, don't forget to leave the front door ajar. Only wear the female undies you found in the briefcase, those you're wearing now, I hope. You'll then lie down on the bed, and wait, wait. Your mistress will arrive to give you what you deserve and more,

Blind Date

fulfilling your wishes for a blind date. A fascinating date since you'll never ever get to see your mistress' face.

After saying this to the man, she got to her feet to put an end to the meeting, and, with utter sangfroid, walked into the crowd – a face among so many other faces – and disappeared; a blot of Pollack, a clipping of Schwitters, a stained and battered mattress.

Once out of the museum, she eagerly breathed in the afternoon air and was happy that the crazy story of the blind date was over for her, at last.

She walked three steps and knew that it wasn't over; no, it had just begun. Now she had to face her own blind date with that unknown part of her self that had gotten her entangled in somebody else's lust.

Michèle Roberts
& *Patricia Duncker*
The Difference of View

LETTER 1

Date Sent: 04 April 2005
From: patricia@penandinc.co.uk
To: michèle@penandinc.co.uk
Subject: My Writing Worlds

Dearest Michèle,

Here I am in the Midi, still bad-tempered, weighed down with a heavy cold and a hacking cough that would have done credit to Emily Brontë. I think we should start with the recent row about women's writing in *The Guardian* (Wednesday 23 March 2005) – 'disappointingly domestic, the opposite of risk-taking . . . depressed as hell' – say Toby Litt and Ali Smith, the editors of *New Writing 13*, just published by Picador. The other adjectives they used were 'melancholy' and 'dull'. That's what women's writing is like and that's why they didn't include anything of that nature in their collection. This description certainly fits a lot of writing on the market, not all of it written by women. I must say I endorsed your riposte to *The Guardian* – there are no intrinsically dull subjects for fiction – the quality of the writing and the treatment of the theme are the measure of the work. In any case, if my memory doesn't fail me, the *Oresteia* trilogy by Aeschylus takes place in and around the House of Atreus and deals with excessively bloody family conflict. Most murders take

The Difference of View

place in domestic space, as do all the major landmarks in our lives, birth, marriage, love, death. The *Oresteia* addresses infanticide, homicide and matricide as affairs of state, profoundly political in their implications for the stability of the social order. But the story is about a family, a family in which they all hate each other even unto murder, but a family nevertheless. The most fabulous sections of Tolstoy's *Anna Karenina* deal with domestic existence – the marriage between Levin and Kitty. This is the other end of passion's scale where Tolstoy's hymn to domestic rural marriage is a religious search for value, a great torrent of rejoicing in the sacraments of everyday existence.

But this isn't what Ali Smith and Toby Litt are going on about, is it? What they're addressing is the fact that what used to be described and denounced as *women's writing* has been shrunken down and circumscribed to 'women's interest fiction'.

I find that it's very helpful to take the long view and to dig deep into literary tradition whenever I'm faced with an artificial row that's almost certainly been concocted to sell a few newspapers. Women's writing, when I was first arguing for its existence and legitimacy over thirty-five years ago, was a raw and savage thing, a register that smashed the old forms, all the old structures which could not contain a woman's anger, vindictiveness and rage. Poetry smeared the pages with subjects never seen before – the rank stench of women's desires and women's dreams. Novels contained mad lists, rhetoric on a Biblical scale, denunciations of politics, philosophy, religion, all religions, linguistics, literature and history. Sacred cows lay in delightful shattered heaps. The unthinkable got said, or rather shouted. Marriage was institutional masochism, children were bloodsucking vultures and the sooner we dashed their brains out on rocks the better. Lesbianism was infinitely sexier than heterosexuality and didn't give you cervical cancer. Women should cease to be the carers of the nation. We should belong to and take care of no one but ourselves. All across the world we should beat our ploughshares into swords, rise up and slaughter all opposition, obliterate the lot of them.

I still like the sound of all this.

One of the essays I read over twenty years ago was Audre

Michèle Roberts & Patricia Duncker

Lorde's *The Uses of Anger*. Anger, she argued, is a fruitful thing, for it gives you information and energy. And that's what writing by the women who were dismantling conventional femininity once had in spades: information and energy. These were new ways of thinking, being, writing, an entire literature and cultural engagement, which once amounted to an heroic adventure into consciousness. Has all this been abandoned and lost?

I don't read much 'women's interest fiction' beyond the odd foray to see if it all remains as disappointingly dull, melancholy, depressed, domestic and linguistically flat as it was when I last called. For this is the writing – usually constructed out of unexamined naturalism and exhausted realist cliché – which offers up a vision of women as perky and game, but emotionally inept, dominated by ideologies of desire, obsessed by their relationships with men, or lack of them, pathetically apolitical, handicapped by the children they nevertheless adore, and faced with tiny dilemmas which assume enormous proportions. Which cushion cover should I purchase? Hard not to dismiss the lot as vacuous late-capitalist claptrap. But this is what most people – women readers as well as men, think that women's writing is. And it sells and sells and sells and sells. Some of this fiction is about what we used to call 'the double shift' – how to have kids, be a sex goddess, manage the domestic front and hold down a full-time, high-flying job. These books are serialized on Radio 4. They are relentlessly middle class and middle brow. I followed one of these serials, mesmerized by triviality. It was called *I Don't Know How She Does It: The Life of Kate Reddy, Working Mother* by Allison Pearson (Chatto & Windus, 2002). Who cares how she does it? Why does she bother? Am I the only woman who asks those questions? The marketing pitch on Amazon.co.uk was terribly clever bilge, and actually addressed to men.

> *She can break your balls. Kate Reddy is tough on men and the causes of men. She will break your heart. Don't read this book in public. People hate to see a grown man cry. You sleep with her. Now wake up to her. What you don't know about women would fill a book. This is that book.*

The Difference of View

Clever, eh? It actually sounds like radical stuff. But men don't read books like this in droves, women do. I bet Pearson sells more than either Ali Smith or Toby Litt put together.

The Utopian rage which I valued so deeply is completely absent in 'women's interest fiction'; so is the linguistic energy. At one end of the spectrum the genre teeters into airport fiction, which usually has a little bit of fucking and menace included at the edges, and may have a pacy plot; at the other end it falls into Aga sagas with uplifting endings. I can't say I've ever finished the airport action-fiction variety, as I forget what happened at the beginning of the sentence before I reach the end. Sometimes long before I even find the verb. Or notice that the verbs are completely missing. And I've never read the last ten pages of either tome by Helen Fielding's *Bridget Jones*. But I have ploughed through many productions by Joanna Trollope, while investigating bestsellerdom. And what makes a 'women's interest' bestseller? Love, love, love – romantic cliché in all its gory nuance.

What's she got against comfort fiction, I hear you cry! It's official. Patricia Duncker is a mad, humourless bitch. Surely we can put our literary feet up from time to time.

Yes, of course we can – and so we should. I think that one of the reasons I still adore reading war stories is because queer passions, the love between men who are comrades-in-arms, gives me more room for fantasy gratification. Will I be the heroic submarine commander with the maternal passion for the young boys in my charge and the bristly relationship with my first officer, who adores me but who challenges my judgement? Or will I be the equally heroic, virile commander of the ship of the line whose men will follow him to death or glory, but whose deepest love is for the doctor, his sole confidant, the man who binds up all their wounds? And believe me, this is comfort fiction with a vengeance. Even the dialogue in submarine novels never changes from book to book. 'Half ahead both, Number One.' The settings are undeniably domestic. Here we all are on board our ship, inside what you would read as 'the maternal body', the belly of the whale. Patrick O'Brien's *Master and Commander* series has quite a strong female following, although it's really a boy's thing. It's even advertised as 'Jane Austen *sur mer.*'

As a woman reader I can occupy every fictional space. And better still run the gauntlet of mortal danger. What are women's adventure stories? What adventures lie in wait for us? How can we find them? How can we be heroes? I want a fiction of heroines who are transgressors in gendered space, women who are straight talkers, radically independent of all conventions and ideologies, women who know their own minds, act on their own desires, women who are duplicitous, cunning, double. Women who can fight, with their fists and words and teeth, women who win, women like us.

All My Love,

Patricia

LETTER 2

Date Sent:	07 April 2005 20:38
From:	michèle@penandinc.co.uk
To:	patricia@penandinc.co.uk
Subject:	in reply to your letter

Dearest Patricia,

If that is how you write when you are ill I wonder how you write when you are well! Some people do stream of consciousness. You do Niagara Falls.

I too am in France. In a small house: a domestic space. That means a cave of making: word salads; soufflés; books; dreams; conversations; love; fires. I connect domestic space back to the Gothic tradition. Interiors were where sexual violence, incest, rape, murder, wife-beating, child-whipping, etc., went on, as Mrs Radcliffe *et al* knew all too well. Charlotte Brontë brilliantly wrestled her Gothic inheritance into her own passionate form of realism. She brought together social reality, fairy tale, myth, Shakespearean nets of metaphor as sub-texts and sub-plots, and

The Difference of View

vitriolic satire. Yes, it's the watered-down, corrupt version of her legacy I loathe, the bad pastiches of Daphne du Maurier, though I love pointing out to snobs who rubbish Mills and Boon as books for stupid women that the bodice ripper has a long, distinguished/disreputable heritage. (I can't read Mills and Boon but women have good reasons, pace Janice Redway, for reading them – it's to ask and answer questions about marriage – if that's your bag – and a good writing exercise is to tear up Mills and Boon novels and porn mags and collage them together in amusing ways.) But one reason I think some people condemn domestic space as a subject/setting for fiction is because the house/home/flat represents the maternal body. Men are supposed to flee it in order to become real men. Women who don't want to be marked as conventionally feminine flee it too. Look at those female heroes of early feminist detective fiction, so proud of themselves for not being able to cook. Yet Roland Barthes once said that writing means playing with the body of the mother. So one's got to transgress those gender codes. (The best writers are often girly boys and mannish girls – conventional masculinity and femininity are perversities.)

The problem resides in the way we use language to split things. Feminism was and is subversive because it challenges those splits and definitions. When I was growing up there were writers and women writers. Real writers (men) and gendered writers (women). Men were People. Women were sexed. Women writers could choose to deny their gender and pretend to be men, or they could accept their gender and write feminine stuff OR they could be feminists and set out to subvert and disrupt all those divisive categories. We seem to have gone back to those bad ole days of rigid gender divisions. It depresses me when we are interviewing for the MA and so few students dare to say they read women writers. Oh, they say, gender doesn't matter – I just happen not to read women. Our culture does not make much space for bold, subversive, experimental women writers. One per generation is supposed to be enough. Angela Carter. Christine Brooke-Rose. Marina Warner. Jeanette Winterson. Lazy journalists refer only to male writers. We get wiped off the literary map. It makes me utterly furious. I remember my dear publisher coming to visit me here in France once. I was fulminating about the injustice of the way that the media only ever mentions the men of our generation and she said: but they're just some guys in a field that's all they are.

There were many sorts of feminism in the seventies: I was with the libertarian socialist carnivalesque lot. We opposed bourgeois feminists who we thought just wanted to get by in a men's world. With the economic changes of the eighties it was feminism-lite, capitalist feminism, that became acceptable: all a girl wants is a pair of shoulderpads and a job in the city and a nanny. The accompanying, suitable women's novels echoed a corrupt version of psychoanalysis made popular by humanistic therapy in the States: just find the problem in your past, face it, and stride forward into your brave new life. Fit into the world. Don't try to change it.

Like you, I find rage and anger energizing. They make me want to break things. We have to break the old forms of novels we have inherited, break old sentences, break clichés. To write I believe we have to sink down into the unconscious, where language dances chaotically, where unacceptable desires and fears surface to challenge us. Then we rise back up again clutching our treasures, find ways to create new forms and new sentences. This is painful and terrifying. It is difficult not easy. But it is the only thing worth doing. I do not respect easy, superficial writing. If I loathe banal 'women's novels' I loathe equally those cool ironic tales some men write, the men terrified of feeling.

However, love as a subject is very interesting, I think. It doesn't just have to mean the search for a husband. That was relevant to Jane Austen's time. Middle-class women absolutely had to find husbands and so she writes about that. Good for her. But love cannot be tamed by marriage. Love is a force, an energy. It can power our writing as well as being our subject. You have to love language ferociously in order to break it, destroy it, play with it, remake it, make new shapes with it. Can you write well if you are indifferent? I have written a lot about sexual love, love between mothers and daughters, love between fathers and daughters, between siblings. Desire makes me begin to write, gives me the courage to keep going, furnishes me with subjects,

The Difference of View

because desire gets so tangled up with all those interesting other emotions like fear, greed, hatred. Like you, I used to enjoy reading novels about male heroes, partly because when Hornblower, for example, wasn't steering his ship between sandbanks or coping with mutinies, he was dealing with the passionate Lady Barbara, and I did enjoy being Hornblower and learning how men loved women. Or didn't. One reason I read Georgette Heyer in my teens was that her heroines often cross-dressed, in order to have better adventures, and passed successfully as men, fighting duels with the best of them. Real shape-shifting stuff: while she's dressed in a wig and frockcoat and breeches Prue (in *The Masqueraders*) is described as a slender stripling, but the moment she's back in her hoops and petticoats she's 'a big woman'. I've spent my writing life investigating that word woman, and now I am investigating the word man too. Wonderfully slippery: the words dance together and won't stay still. By the way have you read any slash fiction? It's just as you described: women writing and reading about pairs of male adventurers in order to be liberated from gender-corsets.

Now I shall go and build a fire and open a bottle of wine and drink your very good health.

Love from Michèle

Michèle Roberts & Patricia Duncker

LETTER 3

Date Sent:	09 April 2005
From:	patricia@penandinc.co.uk
To:	michèle@penandinc.co.uk
Subject:	Two Sorts of Antibiotic

Dearest Michèle,

I crawled into town yesterday, so ill with bronchitis and miasmas that the whole enterprise was a near-death experience. The pharmacist recommended an excursion to Lourdes. Great – I thought that was for the terminal and the desperate. Maybe I am terminal and desperate. The doctor put me on two sorts of antibiotics and, wait for it, made me write down all the titles of my books in French. 'I love reading,' said he, 'I'm reading this at the moment,' (producing Isabel Allende's *House of the Spirits*) 'do you like her work?' I can't believe this: a Frenchman who reads women writers? He must be an alien visitor from another galaxy doing research. I go through his bookshelf – and look who's here – Marie Nimier, Marguerite Yourcenar, Irène Némirovsky. 'Are you looking for something?' asks the baffled doctor. He is very puzzled when I sit down again and cannot stop smiling. 'I think you are a quite wonderful doctor,' I declare, gazing at him *en plein adoration*. He is enough of a Frenchman to deliver a little bow.

I have been reading some more 'women's interest fiction' to see if I have been too harsh and find that my invective should have been far stronger and more searching, indeed Shakespearean in its rage and intensity. It really is as bad as I feared. The heroine of the book I am reading has given up her career to take care of her loathsome children. She is much envied by her two female friends who went on being high-powered and rich. Everyone is Looking for Love. By which they mean a man to marry or one with whom they can have an affair. And this is how they are represented in the fictions, as man-hungry housecleaning dutiful daughters. It's not the fact of domestic space that is at fault – it's that women who are shunted into the railway siding of

The Difference of View

domesticity become a service industry for men, children, old people, all the halt and the lame left over from the feast. And we, the dissenters, are treated as unnatural hags if we refuse to do it. Leave home. That's the only answer. I write about women who leave home. I leave home myself. Don't be there when the gentlemen call round. Or don't answer the door.

But of course, *women's writing* and the debased forms thereof, have always existed, side by side. This was true in the eighteenth century. For every Ann Radcliffe there were forty Maria Monks, and alongside the massed ranks of flowery poetesses in the mid-nineteenth century there was one Elizabeth Barrett Browning and one Emily Dickinson, locking up her writing in her desk, where it waited, like Sleeping Beauty for someone in some future time, the cross-dressed princesses on horseback galloping through the briars to awaken her with a kiss.

Your comments about feeling – the male writers specifically, who are terrified of feeling, set me thinking. Many writers, male and female, cannot distinguish between sentimentality and passionate, powerful emotion. I often find American writers produce work that is especially problematic either when their themes ensure that they are confronted with emotions or when they are asked to represent them. The result can be something as awful as Alice Sebold's rape-and-resurrection novel, *The Lovely Bones*, which is 'hospital-get-well-card-fiction': inane feel-good sentiment, when we all know that the patient has no chance whatsoever of recovery. One writer who does deep feeling quite wonderfully is Tobias Wolff. I read *Old School*, which is a literary masterpiece about growing up, writing, class, loyalty, envy, writers' lives, the love between us and the lies we tell ourselves. These are all the big subjects. My big subjects too. I soaked my brain in Wolff's excellent prose, which is finely wrought, yet utterly simple, subtle, translucent. I found the following passage, which is of the deepest interest to us both:

Michèle Roberts & Patricia Duncker

For a writer there is no such thing as an exemplary life. It's a fact that certain writers do good work at the bottom of a bottle. The outlaws generally write as well as the bankers, though more briefly. Some writers flourish like opportunistic weeds by hiding among the citizens, others by toughing it out in one sort of desert or another.

The life that produces writing can't be written about. It is a life carried on without the knowledge even of the writer, below the mind's business and noise, in deep unlit shafts where phantom messengers struggle toward us, killing one another along the way; and when a few survivors break through to our attention they are received as blandly as waiters bringing more coffee.

No true account can be given of how or why you became a writer, nor is there any moment of which you can say: This is when I became a writer.

I loved his image of the lift shafts into the unconscious, and the rising phantoms. This is a pure horror movie metaphor; the thing struggling towards you through the dark canyons of the mind, killing as it rises towards the light, retaining its link with the abyss, the thing of darkness I acknowledge mine. I think we both agree that writing, the best writing that we can ever make, comes from the deepest places, even the places we hesitate to acknowledge, the places we fear. But then we welcome these phantom messengers into our domestic space and live with them, often cheerfully enough, for the writing time it takes to make art. We are oddly enough, very close indeed to Coleridge's distinction between Fancy and Imagination: the Imagination is the primordial spirit, the summoning into being, the great *I am*, whereas Fancy is that secondary shaping power, the ability to present that thing of darkness to an audience and give the beast a local habitation and a name.

But how do we see ourselves – as writers who are women? I share your anger at the way in which we, as women writers who take our work seriously and neither apologise for what we do, nor diminish its importance, are too often patronized, dismissed or ignored. I'm not underestimating the difficulty. Our culture will

The Difference of View

always praise and reward the writers who endorse rather than disturb its values. But we are not marginal to this written world. We are at its core. Our methods are oblique, but our presence is perpetual. Nor are we alone. I look along the shelf in front of me: A. S. Byatt, Alison Fell, A. L. Kennedy, Rose Tremain, Janet Davey, Lucy Ellman, Jenny Newman, Helen Dunmore, Ruth Padel, Selima Hill, Claire Messud. The next generation is there too: Simonetta Wenkert, Marie Darrieussecq. And these are only the ones I can see. There are entire bookshelves next door. In the late 1970s Mary Jacobus wrote an essay about Charlotte Brontë's *Villette* called 'the difference of view'. She argued that there was a radical sexual difference in writing by women, a different interpretation and understanding of the order of things; a different view of sex, religion, history – a difference in desire. I am astonished at how huge the gulf remains between my view of the world and that of my students and my colleagues – even the people who are close to me. I don't think we even agree on what is considered right and good. What price morality and ethics if the abyss lies between us?

But I now believe that this precious 'difference of view' is something that has to be chosen. It is a privilege that we can seize with both hands if we have the courage to do so. We can choose to be collaborators, spineless doormats, conformists, brainless bimbos. We can even choose to be bad writers. The novelist Linda Leith once pointed out to me that it takes a hell of a lot of time, energy and commitment to write a bad book, so you may as well go the second mile and try to write a good one. Every woman has a choice, however small. You can say no, just the once. You can refuse to simper, smile, agree, refuse to follow the crowd. Or you can make the big choice, embrace that 'difference of view', and leave home.

Fiction is like shadow boxing – a shifting argument I conduct not only with different parts of myself but with the books I have read and which continue to haunt me. But I can't stand sitcom fiction or trivial laments about failed heterosexual relationships, or growing-up novels with added child abuse and undiluted whinge. Been there, done that, read the slogans on the T-shirts. I want to read argumentative, difficult fiction, fiction in which the writer has invested the deepest parts of herself, fiction which presents ideas as well as characters and insists on its own axe-grinding agendas. And why not?

All My Love,

Patricia

LETTER 4

Date Sent:	27 April 2005 20:38
From:	michèle@penandinc.co.uk
To:	patricia@penandinc.co.uk
Subject:	in reply to your letter

I waited a while, dearest Patricia, before replying to your last message. I wanted to think about it for a while. One of the seductions of email is its immediacy and speed. It becomes addictive. A response to a loved person shot off, one is quickly left empty, yearning for more. The fix must come faster and faster. Email can make me feel like a starving baby, screaming with hunger, convinced that food will never return. Whereas letters, good old-fashioned letters, take their time, and I have confidence in the *facteur* (or, currently, the *factrice*) that the letter *will* arrive, that love will return, we will be given to and satisfied. Remember how Lucy Snowe in *Villette* yearns for the post to arrive, in case Graham Bretton has written to her? People today yearn like that for emails and text messages. To me they are like junk food; fun now and again; but for delight I want the good bread of letters. I was thinking about *Villette* because it ends with Lucy being given a house, a small and delicate house like a dolls' house, as though she is a child and Paul Emanuel, her benefactor, a good father. (He feeds her well, too, all through the novel, and so one thinks aha! this is the man she will love.) Lucy's house comes complete with balcony, tiny sitting room, miniature kitchen, but it also, crucially, contains a classroom. It is the place

The Difference of View

where she will work, and open a school. So for me domestic space is where I work and cook and rejoice in having healed that traditional split between body and mind. My best house is always the book I am writing; my paper house. The paper tent I can fold up and carry in my pocket and put up anywhere. To become writers we all have to leave home and go on a quest. Into the dark forest we must plunge, and make our own path through. Then, in the centre of the clearing, we come upon the witch's cottage, and lo! inside it there is Colette making soup, making bread, making love, making trouble, making a new book.

The postman here in France is intrigued by how many Brits come out and start doing up the old farmhouses. Male domesticity: plastering and rewiring. We discuss the Freudian angle on this, the reparative act of the child restoring the maternal body damaged by the child's angry fantasy. Then we both start laughing and the postie roars off.

Your Tobias Wolff quotation was fascinating, and probably true, and also seemed to me couched in romantic and masculine terms and why not? I know lots of male writers who think like that, who do not want to think about where their art comes from, preferring to perceive it as Over There, like a faraway planet. I sometimes wonder whether this isn't a metaphor drawn from biology (Freud again – sorry). Fathers cannot be sure their children are their own, whereas mothers have felt the child kicking and dancing, have given birth. So lots of the women writers I know are quite happy to talk about the origins of their art. Sometimes we feel like men and sometimes like women, perhaps (cf. Virginia Woolf on the androgynous imagination). When an image first stirs, you do feel astonished: where on earth did that stranger come from? It's alien, it starts to haunt you like a ghost, it stirs you up and scares you. Then you get to know it, as you say. You try to speak to it. To connect to it. I think of the imagination sometimes as like a silver lasso in our hands, a rope of desire and fear, whirling things back to us. Sometimes the imagination is inside me, my belly full of delicious food. Sometimes it's like a compost heap, seething quietly away, and

Michèle Roberts & Patricia Duncker

you just have to leave it alone to rot down a bit. But you can keep chucking things into it. Sometimes it's that cave in the forest, rich with treasure, guarded by my sleeping dragon-self, perhaps the part of me that is scared of writing for fear of what mad hungers I'll rouse.

Those books we dislike can perhaps be characterized through their form: a kind of worn out social realism dealing in a conventional and clichéd way with personal and domestic problems. Remember how Angela Carter scorned the British novel as a kind of etiquette book? Class issues. How to behave but still get what you want. The novel did originate, of course, in the problem pages of eighteenth century magazines: how to deal with the sexual double standard (still there today in school playgrounds – slags or bitches, whores or madonnas), win through, get a man. *Plus ça change?* You can always be a nice lady in your life if you really want to, and you can indeed attempt to be truly loving and generous and kind, but when you write fiction I think you should be a rebel and you must of course stare unflinchingly at what you do not like. You must subvert the givens of our culture as you subvert the language and your inherited form. Form is the crucial issue, I think. Recently I have been a judge for *The Independent*'s Foreign Fiction Award (as you were two years ago) and what was exhilarating was to read novels which experimented so radically with form. You felt your choices as a novelist opening out and blossoming. Perhaps we should start teaching philosophy in our schools, as the French do. Help students find a strong language for discussing form.

Avanti populo! La lotta continua! Er, that's it.

All my love

Michèle

Old School by Tobias Wolff
Copyright © Bloomsbury Publishing plc
Used by kind permission

simon@pform.co.uk

Ron Butlin
Kindness

Men became dogs, Alice had decided. From day one of Frank's retirement, he'd been perpetually *in attendance*: the domestic pet – always wanting to be talked to, listened to, patted, played with . . . and quite unable to do anything on his own. She'd loved him still – even more as she saw how vulnerable, how helpless almost, he became. Especially at the end. Probably because today is the only day of the week that matters any more, and she's about to go out, Alice finds herself expecting him – in his hat, coat and polished shoes – to be at the front door, hoping to be taken for a walk.

She's just finished giving her hair a last minute brush. Of course Frank *can't* be there – and it would be weakness, plain and simple, to glance down the corridor to check. For several seconds she stands quite motionless in front of the mirror, wanting to whisper his name. But stops herself. Why? No one's watching. So why shouldn't she let her lips move as they clearly long to, and say *Frank*, out loud? Why on earth shouldn't she? There's no one in the house but her, as she knows only too well.

*

If Alice can be said to have a hobby, it's Special Offer Day at the local supermarket. As she turns the corner of the street, she begins speeding up. In addition to 'Giveaways for the Greenhouse', this week's Special Offer leaflet has promised 'a Christmas tree to last a lifetime' and an 'energy-saving miracle': a portable shower unit that allows the used water to be

Kindness

recirculated thanks to a handpump attachment. Sonya, her green bore of a daughter, will be getting it for her birthday, and liking it.

'Mrs Williams?'

A car has drawn up beside her.

'Going into town, Mrs Williams?'

It's Helen Miller. Her husband Michael – six foot of awkward silence broken only by a growl of moustache – is driving. A kindly man, though. They are a kindly couple.

'Only to the supermarket.'

'Like a lift? It's a warm day.'

'It's not far. I can manage, thank you.'

'Of course you can, Mrs Williams. We just thought . . .'

Being sure to take in both Millers and the family moustache in one overall smile, she leans towards the car: 'It's kind of you, but if I'm still moving I know I'm still alive!'

A few more smiles are batted back and forth before Alice can continue on her way.

She spends nearly an hour in the supermarket. Special Offers take time. . . . Finally she settles on the extendible Christmas tree with a pointed metal tip (safety cap attached), for the bubble-wrapped angel (enclosed), and the shower unit. She also buys some meat and vegetables.

At the checkout she asks if she can leave her purchases and pick them up on her way back from the baker's. No problem.

She's hardly gone twenty yards when she hears someone calling after her: 'Old lady! Old lady!'

Naturally she keeps going.

A teenage boy in supermarket uniform comes running to catch up with her. He's holding out her bags: the foodstuffs in one, the shower head sticking out of the other and the Christmas tree under his arm like a rolled up umbrella.

'Your things. I thought maybe you'd forgotten – I mean, maybe you had . . .' He stops, in confusion.

'The girl said she'd keep them for me.' She manages a reassuring smile: 'But that was very kind of you. Thank you.'

The boy nods. Then blushes.

'I'll pick them up shortly,' she explains, 'on my way back from the baker's.' Smile number two's an effort. Much tireder suddenly, she carries on into town.

A warm day and getting warmer. By the time she reaches the next block, she feels that every step's a step further from home. She needs to rest for a few moments, she needs some shade. Eventually she reaches the awning outside Aladdin's Cave, that treasure house of household novelties: full of Special Offers, and tempting as sin. Though what does sin matter to her any more? If there was a God, she'd decided at Frank's funeral, then He had a hell of a lot to answer for. Mysterious ways, right enough. As she stood at the open graveside, almost two years to the very day and as hot, she'd found herself counting up all those wasted Sunday mornings, and all that wasted collection money. And for what? Helplessly she'd watched Frank's last desperate efforts to crawl up a slope that just got steeper and steeper; his screaming and weeping with pain; the drugs, the plastic tubes and oxygen; bits of him packing up one organ at a time, bits of him rotting while she could do nothing but sit there, and look on.

As they'd walked back to the cemetery gates the minister had turned to her: 'Your husband will be at peace now, in a better place.'

Her sudden fury: 'I want Frank *here*, with me!'

The touch of the minister's hand on her shoulder: 'God is Love and Mercy. Let us remember that Our Lord Jesus Christ, His only begotten Son, was sacrificed that we –'

'A few hours on the cross was nothing to what my man had to suffer this last year.' Shaking herself free: 'His whole life, and *that*'s what it came to. If God planned it, he should have thought of gas chambers – would have been kinder.'

The minister's face and neck were already red raw, she was pleased to notice, and showed the promise of a nasty looking sunburn: 'Mrs Williams! You don't know what you're saying. You're angry, you're distressed. I understand. God understands and –'

That was when she'd walked off.

The following Sunday she'd gone to a car boot sale instead. Her first. For the fiver she'd have put into the collection she came home with a cuckoo clock that turned out to announce the

Kindness

hours quite at random. Sometimes the cuckoo remained silent for a whole day then made up for it with a burst of mechanical shooting out, then in, then out again while screeching at full pitch till his spring wound completely down. She nailed his little wooden house up in the hall. Wind him up, she thought, and the poor demented thing at least did his best – which was more than she could say for God.

It's cool under the shop awning. She's in no hurry and can allow herself a comforting glance into the window of Aladdin's Cave: the elephant-shaped teapot that pours out through its trunk, the Eiffel Tower toast rack, the mosque-shaped alarm clock...

'Mrs Williams, how pleased to see you.'

'Good day, Ash.'

'Long time no look round. Welcome, please.'

'No thank you. Just window shopping today.'

'You're tired. One minute, please. I bring a chair.' Before she can stop him he's disappeared into the shop.

What's she to do? She doesn't want to sit down, to be fussed over, to be stared at by every passer-by, but she can't just walk away... Or can she?... But what about the next time she passes his shop? Or will she always have to go the long way round?

'Sit please.'

Ash has unfolded a garden seat for her. She sits down.

'Thank you, you're very kind.' She's having to force out the words.

'A glass of water?'

She's not a *memsahib*, is she? Ash is simply being friendly, she reminds herself, *she*'s the one seeing him as a deferential clasp of hands, a bow and a turban. What's the matter with her today?

She smiles: 'No thank you, Ash. I'll be fine in a minute. Busy, are you?'

'Busy, yes. But troubled also. Every morning I say let there not be trouble – no Paki-calling, no broken windows,' he looks down at the pavement between them, 'and worse things.'

Her hand's resting on the chair arm – very comfortable. The difficulty's going to be getting herself up and beginning the walk to the baker's before the long trek home.

34

Ron Butlin

'I'm sorry to hear that.' She shakes her head, 'Even around here . . .?'

'Here, everywhere. Not skinheads any more. Nice people can be not so very nice.'

Beyond the edge of shade the street is all glare, a harshness of light cut into strips of hot pavement and hot road; when cars come round the corner, their windscreens catch the sun with a stab of sudden brightness. The very thought of walking out again into that heat. . . . She must have nodded off. Only for a few seconds surely. Ash is looking at her, clearly waiting for her to say something.

'You've been very kind, Ash. Thank you.' She gets to her feet. 'I really must be getting back. My daughter's expecting me.' The lie comes easily. 'Goodbye, Ash.' She steps into the heat and drags herself away.

'Don't forget your change, dear.'

The casualness of the assistant's tone hits her like a blow across the face, the kind of blow to make her eyes water. Or is she about to burst into tears? Not tears, she wills herself, not in public. She takes the money and blunders out of the shop, letting the door slam behind her.

What a state she's got herself into. . . . Better to calm down, take a deep breath, eyes straight ahead, left foot forward, right foot. . . . Avoiding Ash's shop, she'll go back into the supermarket, collect her stuff, then home.

Only a dozen or so yards down the road – and she's halted. The bread. With all that mix-up over the money she's gone and left the wrapped loaf on the counter.

She hesitates, but can't go back. Why doesn't one of the customers come out after her? She's ready to smile and to be grateful – and this time really mean it.

'Can I help you . . .?'

A girl of about ten is standing beside her: blonde hair, untroubled blue eyes gazing into her face. Not the least bit shy. 'Can I help you across the road?'

'No, thank you. I was just –'

Already the eyes have veered away to one side: 'If you're fine,

Kindness

then . . .' The girl's walking off.

A split second later, Alice calls after her: 'Just a minute!' For here's the solution to her problem: a girl so blonde, blue-eyed and brimming with kindness will surely be only too happy to go back to the baker's for her.

'Just a minute, little girl! Please!'

A bus goes roaring past. The girl's continued up the street. Too late.

The energy-saving shower in one bag, meat, vegetables and supermarket bread in the other, and the extendible Christmas tree (angel enclosed) tucked under her arm, Alice trudges up to the pedestrian crossing. By edging sideways she's managed to press the button with her elbow, the sign beneath lights up: WAIT. Well, she's waiting. In less than five minutes she'll be home. Which is just as well: if she has to come out with one more *thank you, I'm so grateful / thank you, you're so kind* she'll be screaming it at them. Between that, and her tiredness, and the heat. . . . She can imagine the coolness she'll soon be stepping into at home. She'll lock the front door behind her, change into her indoor clothes, make a pot of tea, switch on the radio. And relax.

No other pedestrian in sight. No traffic either.

She's about to cross when she feels the supermarket bag's handle beginning to stretch. That's the last thing she needs. She takes a firmer grip.

Pip-pip-pip: the lights change to the green man. A car, a sporty-looking piece of red flash thud-thudding with music, has been forced to brake hard and stop. Out of the corner of her eye she sees the driver – shaved head, or maybe bald, and oval, like a peanut. He's glaring at her. Let him.

You've got a lot more time ahead of you than I have, she wants to yell at him. Instead, as she steps off the pavement, exhaustion sweeps over her. The other side of the road seems impossibly far. The heat from the car bonnet's like an oven door standing open. Her left foot, then her right. . . . With Frank beside her, walking to the shops together, walking home together, spending the day together, and the day after. . . . With Frank, without Frank. . . . Her left foot, then her right . . .

36

Ron Butlin

'Hey there, missus!'

The *thud-thud*'s been abruptly turned down and the driver's shouting at her. She feels so tired that if she stops to turn and look, she'll collapse into a heap on the road. So, so tired: her left foot forward, and then her right . . .

The voice, like a lash cutting across her back: 'Come on, grandma, the lights have changed. Move it!'

Her left foot forward, and then her right . . .

Again the lash: 'Move it, I said!' And yet again: 'Your old man'll be waiting for his dinner!'

Suddenly the lash feels like a charge of electricity, a bolt of pure energy that surges through her. She wheels round to face him: 'You – you – Peanut-head!' She puts down her bags.

A double-decker's passing only a few feet away. She ignores it.

Peanut-head revs his engine: 'Come on, missus. The lights. Out the road!'

She's extended this week's Special Offer to its full length, holding it out in front of her like a lance. She's removed the safety cap. Its steel tip flashes in the sun. She takes aim:

'Merry Christmas!' Then rams it in full force.

Peanut-head's leaning out of the window.

'What –? What are you doing, you old bat?'

A final twist for luck. Then, as she pulls it out, there's a rush of escaping air. A most pleasing *hiss*.

A moment later, Alice has stepped lightly onto the opposite pavement. She pauses for a moment to enjoy a last, satisfying look: the long line of stalled traffic is getting longer by the second. Some drivers are hooting their horns, some are shouting and waving their fists. Peanut-head's standing beside his car, staring down at his flat tyre.

She takes a good grip of her bags, turns and strides briskly off.

At her front door she gets out her key. She knows she was definitely in the wrong. Such ingratitude, after all the kindness the world has shown her. She shakes her head, she's beginning to feel sorry for what she's done. Only a little sorry though.

The key turns and her front door opens. She's home.

simon@pform.co.uk

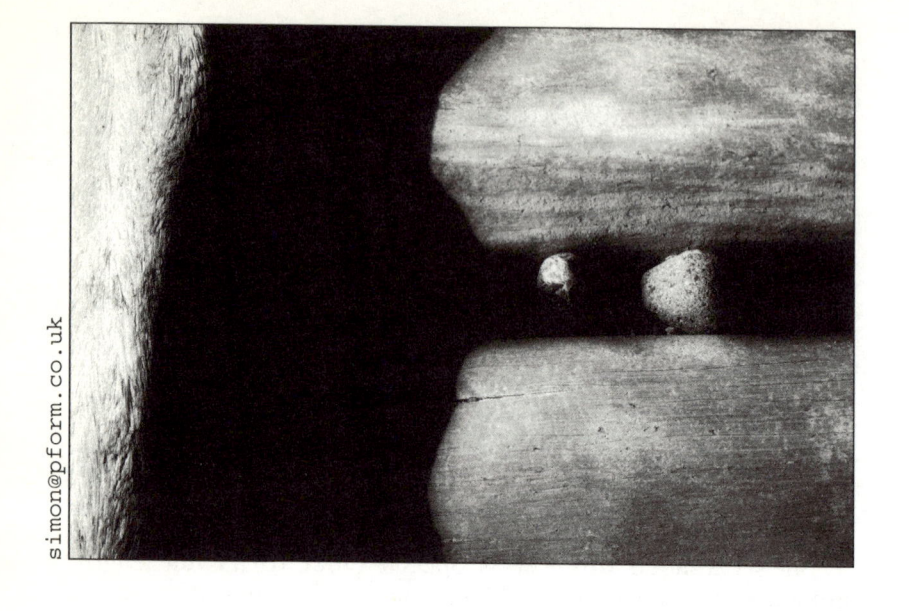

David Solway
Four Poems

THE GARDEN
Lyke as the Culver on the bared bough
— Spenser, Amoretti, 89

Under the pale lilac bush
moorgrass whispers from its hidden bed
to the monarch-bearing milkweed,
and the plump robin freighting
the berry-cumbered honeysuckle
whistles the secret to the chickadee
darting between the hedges.

Laden with epistles
a tumult of bluets and fritillaries
prints the air with messages
as mullein leans its slender stalk
to confide in a tigering of bees
busy with their blacks and golds
and the honey of their living.

Even purple loosestrife
races across the lower meadow
panicked by the yellow trumpets
of the brassy, orchestral lilies,
and the wood dove creaks with fright
for the cover of the branches.

Now the hummingbird,
milking petalled flocks of lavenders and pinks,
stalls in mid-maneuver
while the double-decker dragonfly
in the aftermath of rain
hovers by the spires of the bull thistle,
murmuring its encyclicals
of desire and regret
for the wet and shimmering kingdom.

For the news has spidered out
in the cold opulence of its silks
to every corner of the garden:
to where the tender seed heads
of the ditch-green sedges
purple toward the future
and the ovals of the rosehips
ripe with orpiment
pour their hearts out in the plummeting sun.

For the word has gone out
to all the tremulous creatures
beneath the parable of the white pines
dropping their soft sickles
in russet masses to the ground.
The word has gone out
in the colloquies of those who love the garden
that in the radiant vacancies they inhabit
there is only the gardener
to love them back.

David Solway

What Makes a Poem

The barley
   and the manner of its malting
   its standing up to the wind
   its sprouting and drying
   its gradual ripening

The water
   and the manner of its flowing
   traces of peat and mineral
   its floral and honey notes

The mash tun
   and the manner of the yeasting
   where malt and water mix
   starch turning to sugar
   the draining of the wort

The still
   and the manner of its tending
   its shape – column or pot –
   the ancient skill of the coppersmith

The cask
   and the manner of its keeping
   the flavors of the wood
   the subtle art of the cooper
   its tempering of sublimities

Time
   and the manner of its passing
   of its passing

The maltmaster
   and the manner of his knowing
   the manner of his loving
   the grain, the water, the copper, the wood,
   and the slow ferment of years.

David Solway

COUNTING THE WAYS

How do I love you, but past all pretense.
I love you better than Elizabeth
loved her man, for all her sonnet's elegance.
I love you in excess of my own myth
of me as Giovanni's very self.
I love you more than scholars love their books
arrayed like rich cosmetics on the shelf,
and more than prima donnas love their looks.
I love you, too – though it has now become
unfashionable to talk of all one feels –
as I once did the counterspeech of wit.
I know the heart's a simple sort of drum,
yet love you more than eloquence conceals
or silence that, some say, best utters it.

The Piano in the House in the Woods

The house was in the middle of the woods,
a two-mile footpath through the bush
the only way to get there. You hiked in summer,
strapped snowshoes on in winter, moving in
through birch and pine as silver and as green
as fish scales trapped in ice. But we know all
about the house, how it was built and why
and who worked his fingers down
to fit one plank upon another plank.
We know less about that vintage piano,
how they hauled it through forest and brush,
wedged it through the narrow door much too small,
set it there among a crowd of rockers, tables, sofas.
We know less about that crazy piano,
scratched and dented and out of tune,
than we know of house and woods together.
Unless we say the piano had always
been there, and they built the house around it.

Richard Beard
Honey, I Shrunk the Planet
A Sermon

If you want your version of the world published, make every effort to get to know her, and you know who *she* is, because she used to sleep with *him*, and that bastard's married to the sister of the commissioning editor. But don't tell him he's a bastard, obviously. Let him know he glows in the dark because word gets around, and you know what? It's a small world.

Supposedly. This is one model of the literary life, as a self-serving hive of coteries and changeable alliances moving from one generation to the next, a network of exclusive intimacies. This must be highly reassuring if you're in on it, of it, a node on the trembling web. This model does, however, miss out one essential factor of the literary experience. The actual production of literature.

The problem lies in the choice of metaphor. The buzzy, busy hive, the connecting web, the small world. None of these comparisons seem very helpful when now as always the most distinctive feature of a writer's life is solitude. You are about to set out alone on the adventure of, say, a novel. Ambitious for the work you're about to create, you have the idea that it should contain the world and everything in it, and at this point in the journey, only just out of your depth, the combination of solitude and ambition will make that world seem vast.

Hardly surprising, then, that it's tempting to grasp for a lifeline, any offer of rescue to a smaller and safer place. One shrivelling possibility has it that only a small and select number of people can help. If you can find them, and ingratiate yourselves to the right names in the right order, then all will be well. It will not.

The smallness of the writer's world is best measured in metric,

Honey, I Shrunk The Planet

and not in people. The real challenge of shrink-to-fit (remembering you're still alone) is the process of putting everything you know and ever thought important onto blank sheets of paper. An A4 page measures 210 millimetres by 297 millimetres. For a shortish novel of about 200 typescript pages, the uncharted regions therefore cover an area 59.4 metres by 42. This is about two-thirds of a soccer pitch or the deck area of a small container ship. Small or vast? Depends what you have to say.

Faced with this expressionless expanse of paper, a coterie will not save you. You're about to embark on a solo journey, and need more precise an idea of what it might be like. Let's stick with journeys, now we've started, but what type? One with a terribly long way to go, but not by air, because there's not enough detail to be seen from the windows. Some novels, nevertheless, take a flight path, and the narrow view through scratched perspex is unengaged and distant, an indistinctness of flattened mountains and muddy brown rivers. The journey isn't pedestrian, either, because it needs more pace than that. If you walk, it'll take for ever, but some writers, too, have walked it. Sometimes with interesting results.

I used to think it most like a journey that was also a test of endurance. The Tour de France came to mind. France is a believably big country, if you're on a bicycle, a world in itself of dips and rises, fast stretches with a following wind and long sapping flatlands. The Tour was undeniably bracing, occasionally convivial, and some of the others were on drugs. Understandably so, because the race was long and hard and you had to keep on keeping on, all while saving most of your soul for the inevitable suffering in the mountains.

This was a model that once closely matched my idea of the psychological processes of writing a novel. Sadly. A sporting analogy appealed to me because of the energy required, and the sacrifices to be made in return for glory. There was merit simply in taking part, or so people said, but corrupted by newspapers and UEA, I must have believed that writing was a competition. The analogy betrayed me. It was a race between men in which a flash of champions take the prizes and the rest are condemned to the pack, anonymous *domestiques* who fetch and carry and add to the spectacle without much troubling the podium.

Richard Beard

Wrong. Novel writing makes the Tour de France look easy, and sociable. There will be more numerous and daunting obstacles than the predictable geography of France, and much further to travel. The boundaries of France are simply not broad enough to cope with the ambition of a book, begun in good faith, which refuses to make the world any smaller than it is.

Analogy, the first resort of frauds and prophets, is a rhetorical attempt to make the world more manageable. It ravels consoling connections from an otherwise large and chaotic existence. *Writing a novel is like riding the Tour de France.* If so, that's one less experience in this suddenly smaller world that needs to be understood on its own unique terms.

Fortunately, analogy is an elemental magic: it also makes the world bigger. You have something in mind and the analogy makes you think of something else, which makes you think of something else and so on, images to the power of infinity. Association leads to association until the world has once again insisted on its proper size and shape. Not small, but bigger than any one person can imagine. Hence the difficulty of writing a novel.

If literature *were* a race (old habits die hard), it would be more like the Vendee Globe, which pits solo sailors against each other in a circumnavigation of the planet. Each sailor is alone, and this is not a spectator sport that will be dominating Sky Sports 1 anytime soon. There are hundreds of miles between placings. Even though they're engaged in the same basic activity, and heading in the same general direction, each boat is separated by widely differing conditions and latitudes, everyone in their own localized weather system with their own particular difficulties. The fastest are miles ahead, and you'll never catch them unless their keels fall off. (If you like this analogy, and you do insist on racing, take heart from several recent examples of keels falling clean off. Watch the debris float by. How delicious.)

But there again, it's not a race against other people, nor even against the clock. Books are rarely better for being finished quicker. Ellen MacArthur, my novelist of the year and a surprise omission from the Orange Prize shortlist, reminded every oceangoing writer of the significance, in her memorable phrase, of grunting up. There's also nothing wrong with a good whinge from

47

time to time. But although the journey will be as challenging, and as long over the water, not everyone is a Dame Ellen and can finish a book in 72 days, close to the conceivable minimum.

Most of us will embark with a less brittle determination to get there quickly, but equally determined to get round, and bring something back, and not to give up on the way. Why? As the magic realist Sir Francis Chichester once said, 'because it intensifies life'.

There are certain unavoidable features of the journey whoever you are, whoever you know. It's going to be a long haul, and most people need a fair wind to get started. It's open to both men and women, and the trip has no favourites. You can start from anywhere, it doesn't matter, but you're more likely to make it if you're properly prepared. It does help, for example, to have a competent and sympathetic shore crew. Ellen had her long range weatherman and satellite navigator, her agent, editor, and a supportive Mum and Dad. She made detailed plans in advance, and considered a course in Creative Writing or English Literature as a basic Global Positioning Device. All this must have helped, and you can take maps galore – *How to Write the Knox-Johnston Way* – but they won't make the trip for you. At some point you have to let go, and cast out alone into the silence.

Whatever its exact dimensions, the world is the same size wherever you start. How much you see and record of it is now up to you, but we all cover the same territory sooner or later, crossing and recrossing in the wake of others, or in the memory of their wakes, reliving and hopefully re-inventing every previous attempt to encompass the world we live in. The journey is similar for everyone, and yet also never exactly the same. No two routes will be identical, no matter how many times the journey is attempted. Choose your own route, any route you like; more plausibly, any route you can. Include some stop-offs, go back on yourself, wander lost for years. Just wander.

Some days will be clement and not as hard as you thought. At other times, making headway will be more desperate and impossible than you ever imagined. There will be exhilarating typhoon-force surges, long days in the doldrums, and the unrelenting persistence of the Southern Ocean where progress is only made by defeating the fear that you may not make it. Be

Richard Beard

ready for unexpected obstacles, as well as entirely predictable hazards like the famous enemies of promise – freak storms, rudder malfunction, sudden whales in the hall. You will have to be courageous beyond dreaming and inspired by a vision of the finish, of closing the circle, of having seen and crossed the globe. You have seen it with your own eyes. You have got it all in.

There is a romantic element to the journey that will not fade, no matter how many marketing meetings and sales reports clutter the fanciful ocean. There are uncharted islands to be discovered, even now, and if the world were so small the journey would surely be simpler. You'd never wonder what you were doing here, or lose sight of land. You wouldn't cherish the grand adventure, always worth the candle.

Not everyone is interested, of course. There's the plain fact that to many if not most people round-the-world sailing doesn't matter in the least. It's a minority interest, but what it means to other people is not always the most urgent consideration. Gaze at the long horizon and revel in going solo, you and your sense of destination and your loyalty to your own standards. Believe in the value of the journey in itself, even if it remains, at heart, like poor magnificent Ellen's, unnecessary and possibly irrelevant. But immensely worthwhile if you're the one actually doing it.

So it's not a race, but there's still a finish line, the point at which you've been around the world and closed the circle. It's invisible, and you could miss it. You could stop short, or go too far, yet there is, always, a correct, invisible, flawless place to stop.

'It's great that I can finally switch my brain off and relax in the company of others which I've really missed,' said 28-year-old prizewinning novelist Ellen MacArthur. 'I feel absolutely exhausted but I'm elated to be here. It has been an unbelievable journey.'

You're back. You step outside and look around. Oh no. You haven't moved from where you started. Around the world we go, alone in search of its wonders, and in real time when it comes to an end we're still in Falmouth, or wherever else it was we started. This anti-climax might almost persuade you to accept the limiting smallness of the proverbial small world. Almost. Except with the creases at the corners of your eyes, and your 200 pages of navigated paper, you now know better.

<Image: Come And Be My Baby - Jeremy Webb>

Errol Scott
The Silk Road Chandlery

Wilbert leaned up against the dusty shop door, same as yesterday. A set of pliers and the pulley he was fixing hung limply in his hands at his sides. Behind him, the gorilla angel cleaned her feathers with her front hand-feet.

Over on a filthy desk by the back display cases, the book keeper, Sìlù, was ironing his underwear, his nose just inches from the point of the hot iron. His spine curved beneath the weight of the gorilla angel perched on the back of his neck.

Wilbert looked out past his fringed shop awning to the sapling in the sand by the curb. The dirt road before him inscribed the outermost arc of the oasis town of Aksu. To Wilbert's right stretched the Taklamakan, desert of final death. To his left lay the road to Kashgar market town and beyond that the foothills of the Karakoram Mountains.

'That a leaf or a bird?' asked Wilbert, peering at the sapling's branches.

'Dead leaf,' said Sìlù, the bookkeeper. 'There's needles in my back, I got a fever. Think I'm coming down with dyslexia.'

'It's a balloon!' said the pint-sized angel. 'It's not blown up yet . . .'

She scampered in circles on the bookkeeper's caved-in shoulders. Her eyes were as green as Wilbert's own but her fur was more silvery than Wilbert's blond.

'Sweaty hot – maybe diabetes . . .'

On the grand opening day four years ago, Sìlù had shuffled through crêpe paper streamers into Wilbert's marine shop, his money box banging against his hip. Camel care and ointments,

The Silk Road Chandlery

Sìlù had said, not brass bits and boat parts. I'm right, I'm a bookkeeper and I'm certified.

Las Vegas model, Wilbert had countered, build it and they will come. In five years, fortune in hand, I'll joyride my mountain bike down the Kunjerab Pass, coast with my feet up through the China-Pakistan frontier and then right on out to the ocean; when I hit the water's edge, I'll buy a charter fleet out there. Wouldn't have seen this spot but for the donkey-jam-of-the-century on the market road to Kashgar. Waterfront rent's a killer, couldn't afford it. But here, right here, beside the most famous transport route ever – this is the place for a marine shop. I can feel it.

Despite four increasingly pointed refusals of Sìlù's decreasingly expensive services, the bookkeeper had returned daily. On the fifth day, lugging camel clippers and shiny tubes of grease, Sìlù had moved in and been keeping Wilbert's books ever since. The grease lay in the inventory shed out back; the money box lay on the rickety desk; Sìlù's bile hid in his throat.

'A balloon in Aksu . . .' said Wilbert.

In the distance, Wilbert could see dust puffing up around five cyclists as they slogged along the road into town; they pushed sticky yellow bikes ahead of them, leaving the gruelling desert crossing behind. Every few yards they would stop to compare papers to the hand-painted signs all down the road.

'You talking to who?' Sìlù laid a blacker pair of indescribables upon the flattened original pair.

'The tiny *gandharva*. On your shoulder, right there,' said Wilbert, looking over his shoulder into the marine shop. ''Sgot wings.'

The gorilla angel shifted her weight on the back of the bookkeeper's neck and scratched her ear with a back foot-hand. She sat up, pulled a squashed lump from her satchel and began to peel it.

'No such thing as *gandharvas*, no such thing as angels,' said Sìlù. 'And there's nothing on my shoulder. You're crazy. Crazy!'

'We are NOT!' The gorilla angel bared her fangs and pierced the just-peeled lemon.

The cyclists were getting closer. Wilbert crunched the pulley with his pliers into bicycle brake-clamper shape: Taklamakan sand ground brakes and gears the same way every time. He watched the five cyclists pull up in front of the fringed awning; they checked the last hand-painted 'Silk Road Chandlery' sign posted right on the sapling, then pushed their bikes over to lean them up against the shop front.

'We're a marine chandlery. Winches for your foredeck. No bike parts,' said Wilbert.

'We're closed,' Silù shouted from his low rickety desk at the back of the cedar shelf-lined shop. 'I'm coming down with dyslexia!'

'That make you open then?' asked the tallest cyclist. The rabbit ears on his yellow baseball cap were wilting in the heat. 'You're in the guide book for best bike parts: "Last chance to stock up before the Karakoram Highway Mountains with their highway-nudging glaciers, snow-tipped peaks and heart-stopping views; then pass through Hunza valley, past Lake Tianchi and on to the Kunjerab Pass."'

Wilbert bit his lip. 'Your port-side brake-clamper's blown,' he replied at last. He wiped the pulley on his cotton vest. 'Prevailing winds and grit. This'll do.'

The first cyclist took the crunched pulley and tested it over the rim of his front wheel: it snugged the brake pads against his tyre perfectly.

'Um, my gears are also a bit, er . . .'

'Mine too,' said the second yellow cyclist.

'It's one of the highest mountains passes in the world,' said the fifth. 'Got to have solid equipment to survive the screaming joyride down the Kunjerab.'

Wilbert rubbed his curly head. 'I could rig you up a double-purchase system with a few reefs and some winch parts for gears. Cut your time to distance ratio by five per cent, maybe more,' said Wilbert. He continued with more enthusiasm, 'I'm heading that way too. One day. Then right down to Karachi Harbour, almost saved the funds. Taken me four years. One mighty mega-sale more . . . if I could outfit a proper sized boat with sails fit for a king . . . that'd do it.'

'Taklamakan,' screeched Silù, waving his iron and knocking his no-brim cap askew. 'Southwest corner of the Gobi, desert of

The Silk Road Chandlery

final death. No ships! Camel care'll make funds, big funds in Aksu. Not marine shops!'

The gorilla angel poked her lemon rinds into her satchel and began to snap Sìlù's ears like rubber bands. ('Aack! Anorexia!')

'We passed a king,' said the cyclist with the rabbit ears brightly. 'A desert king with ships. Heading this way, maybe three days behind us.'

'A king with a boat?' asked Wilbert bending a forestay casually around another pulley. 'Did you see what kind?'

'Dunno, never saw 'em. I just talked to the assistant. Better make his sails as big as you can though, he had a bunch of camels and sheep in his entourage. Seemed like a pretty important king.'

'We could make it adjustable...' said Wilbert to his angel. 'It would use up all my sailcloth though. Nothing left for sales to anyone else until next shipment, end of November. Tourist season doesn't begin again till April. What do you think, angel?'

'Who're you talking to?' asked the cyclist. One of his rabbit ears half-perked above his salt-streaked face.

'He's crazy,' hissed Sìlù from the shadowed back corner.

'I think it's a balloon,' said the gorilla angel, preening her leg feathers. 'It's waiting.'

The desert sunrise cracked through the window of Wilbert's marine shop, slithered over the basket of vegetables ripening on the sill and fell down the shelves and shelves of pintles, fairleads, stanchions and stern plugs. It slid past rolls of rope, stacks of tillers and teetering heaps of *Voyaging Under Sail*, *Adventures in Seafood*, and *Simply Celestial: The Complete Navigator's Guide*. It followed the grooves in the carpet to the new market-bought glacier water bottles under Sìlù's desk.

Curly mandarin orange peels hung from Sìlù's ears as he furiously ironed his unidentifiables. Wilbert sat among his floor cushions just inside the front door; he was swishing crimson-tinged paint thinner, lining up labels bearing the caption 'Silk Road Chandlery – All Things Marine' to dry and erasing the red painty footprints from across the knee-high display table in front of him. The gorilla angel was helping: she leaned up against Wilbert, slurping her oranges and purring while he wiped up the table and her red feet.

Errol Scott

'We'll send these labels on the bottles by donkey courier. Like a promotional gift . . . to the desert king,' said Wilbert to the little gorilla. 'He'll get them and know exactly where we are and what we've got.' Wilbert cleared his brushes to one side; he unrolled sheets of sail plans where the footprints had been. 'Silù, we'll need another painted signboard. To announce the "Sail Fit For A King"!'

Silù set his iron on its haunches, stomped over to sweep up Wilbert's old paint pots and brushes from the edge of the display table, then disappeared through the fringed back doorway to the inventory shed; thunderous clanking, then silence ensued.

The gorilla angel lay on her back near Wilbert, exhausted from her artistic efforts. Her fluffy belly rose and fell as she rubbed her furry head and tore open a tomato with her feet. For a whole quiet hour Wilbert scribbled notes on his sail plans.

'The wind on Lake Tianchi is gusty, comes through all the glacier mountains . . . the sail'll need to be deep drafted for light breezes . . . extra grommet rows for reefing . . . Hey!' said Wilbert, looking up. 'That looks like . . . those are my dinner tomatoes!'

'MINE!' screeched the gorilla angel.

She sprang into the air, tomato seeds squirting onto Wilbert's sail drafts and copies of *The Magic of Sail* by the door. She darted over to sink her claws into the back of Silù's neck as he returned from the inventory shed grumbling, 'Dyspepsia!' Silù began nonchalantly ironing his money box, hunched under the weight of the gorilla angel; she was now perched on his neck, trying to extricate tomato seeds from the finger-toes of her hand-feet.

Through the front window, Wilbert could see the dust rising out on the road: four sweaty cyclists on rally-red mountain bikes were reading the new sign that Silù had just knocked into the sapling.

'Sale on? Glacier water fit for a king? Great!' said the first biker through the door.

'Er,' said Wilbert. 'Silù?'

'Super great,' said three more cyclists in curly-brimmed hats, crowding in behind the first with empty pannier bags. 'Fill 'er up!'

'I do my best! Simple mistake!' said Silù from under his desk. He was already passing out water bottles and pocketing a shower of coins.

The Silk Road Chandlery

'He did it on purpose!' said the angel.

'But . . . you do my taxes for two countries,' said Wilbert. 'Tax form wording's way more complicated than signs . . .'

'Mmm. Not much back last year,' said Sìlù, his eyes shifty. 'Or the year before. Terrible. You invest these coins . . . sell camel care ointment! My distributor –'

'On purpose!' screeched the gorilla angel, squeezing her claws deeper into Sìlù's neck and bonking his ear with an eggplant from Wilbert's window basket. 'He stole your tax refunds. Send him packing!'

'Right. We'll get rock pigeons and send the labels to the king by air,' said Wilbert grimly to the angel. 'As there's no bottles left . . .'

He turned to the bookkeeper. 'Take half those coins and get some decent birds from the market. Everyone gets a second chance, Sìlù – but only one.'

Sìlù scuttled out, clinking coins and muttering a medical dictionary or so under his breath; the little gorilla fluttered from Sìlù's hunched neck to Wilbert's shoulder as the bookkeeper passed the display table on his way out the front door. He shook his fist at the dead leaf on the sapling, then disappeared round the corner to the town market.

'We passed a king a while back. Maybe two days behind us . . .' piped up the smallest cyclist. 'Are those brake clamps?'

All afternoon Wilbert and the gorilla angel traced sail curves from Wilbert's blueprints onto his best quality sailcloth. Wilbert snipped sail panels across the carpeted floor on his knees while the angel trailed behind him shredding leftover sail bits between all four of her feet. Purple-red juice dribbled down her chin as she chewed a bit of raw meat that Wilbert was making no inquiries about. Sìlù still had not returned. In front of Wilbert, the floor darkened.

'No more brakes,' said Wilbert over his shoulder, addressing two blue racing helmets and a sequined indigo fez at the door. 'Or winches.'

'No brakes needed – a few more miles and we're on the screaming joyride down the Kunjerab Pass!' said the skinny racing

helmet. 'But some new chains for the uphill would go a long way . . . er, you making cycle sails? Hey, I'll give you double what the last guy gave you if you've got any left –'
'Nope.'
'We're making dinner. Fifteen fen a bowl!' announced Silù from the front steps behind the three cyclists. He held up a basket with five limp lumps and a multitude of shiny tubes. 'Best bargain – and plenty left over for camel ligament salve!'
Wilbert sprang from the floor and advanced past the cyclists ('On purpose!' chanted the angel stamping a hand-foot on the shop floor). Wilbert stood on the doorstep above Silù who held his ground.
'Trained birds only fly *home*! Not to kings. Just dinner birds in the market. You send me to market, you want dinner birds!' said Silù. 'Simple mistake!'
'You'd better pray there's a live bird up in that sapling – and not a miserable leaf,' said Wilbert quietly. 'Or deep in the night, when you least expect it, Silù, I will find you, and then I'm gonna –'
'Always talking to himself,' said Silù, edging past Wilbert and then bolting for his corner. 'Talking, talking. Never acts. He's crazy!'
'How much for the cycle sails?' asked the chubby blue racing helmet.
'These guys are probably the last ones before April,' Wilbert whispered sideways to the angel who had fluttered up from the shop floor to snuggle on his shoulder. 'No water, no pigeons. End of season. The money box is empty and the king'll be here too soon. Cycle sails instead . . . in the long run, it wouldn't be enough. At least, it might not be regular . . . it might take years . . .'
The angel blinked her green eyes and slurped down a raw tail. 'On the plus side, the inventory shed's bulging with enough stock for a dromedary wellness spa.'
'Hmm,' said Wilbert. He shook his head. 'It's not just about being able to buy the charter fleet – the "getting there" has got to be good too. Camel pedicures just aren't . . .' He straightened up. 'No. I need every bit of sailcloth for the king's sail. He'll be here in two days. Two more days will be enough if we go all out . . .'
'We can make it,' the angel whispered back.

The Silk Road Chandlery

Wilbert turned to the cyclists who were now scattered through the shop peering into the display tables which lined the walls. 'How about brass ship bells? Could fix 'em to your handle bars, work wonders in a donkey-jam. Could've done with some myself once –'

'You said "king"?' asked the skinny racing helmet. 'Even with the wind behind us, we barely passed a kind of camel king just outside of Aksu . . . He was making good time! Should be here by tomorrow – might have arrived with us too, except for the sheep.'

'Tomorrow!' said Wilbert. ('Impossible,' muttered Sīlù, smiling to himself.)

'I don't know about a bird up that tree,' said the sequined indigo fez, gazing out the door to the sandy kerb. 'Kinda looks like a balloon to me.'

Wilbert threaded his industrial sail-sewing machine for the first time with the little gorilla purring against his arm. The angel mis-pinned sail seams and got tangled in the batten bag, but panel by panel into the night, the king's new sail unfurled across the display table and over its edge. When the morning sun re-lit Wilbert's marine shop, he was already teaching the gorilla angel to tape batten pockets to the outer edge of the sail to stiffen it. By noon, the pockets were sewn, elasticized, spring-tested; by dusk, the sail's corners were reinforced and all the grommets punched through ('NO! No holes!' wailed the angel; 'They're for reefing,' said Wilbert. 'Too much of a blow and the king can lower it halfway and tie the sail's middle to the boom. It's adjustable, see?').

By late evening, the sail had been pressed, tested, and pinned to the awning: it curved down to the ground, gleaming in the calm night air. Wilbert sat out on the front shop steps watching the angel pounce on mantids in the dust; her satchel bulged with pre-emptive string beans to ward off simple mistakes. Sīlù, however, banished to his corner with no money to count and all his laundry already flattened, refused to look up from polishing his iron. The street in front of the Silk Road Chandlery remained empty and king-free.

'It's beautiful,' said the angel. Her face shone as she gazed up at the mighty sail.

Errol Scott

'Doesn't know we're here, probably doesn't have a guide book,' said Wilbert. 'Getting too dark to even see it if you're not right up close . . .'

The little gorilla crunched the last leg of a mantid in her teeth. 'We need a fire, right here, a big one,' she said. She scuffled a shallow depression in the dirt by the path's edge. 'He's got to see it. He'll come.'

'A bonfire,' said Wilbert, standing up. 'Big enough to be seen all over Aksu!'

Wilbert hauled the bag of leftover sail cloth snippings out to the edge of the gorilla's fire pit and dumped it in. He piled on every package wrapper and pristine copy of *Yachting World* from the back inventory shed for kindling. Wilbert lit a match; the sail cloth coughed and wheezed.

Wilbert picked up the few parched sticks in front of the shop and pitched them into the fire. He threw on non-king battens and books and oars. He dumped all the metal boat parts from the cedar shelves lining the marine shop and then tore the shelves off the walls to add to the blaze. The little gorilla up-ended a satchelful of shrivelled leaves on the pile (her string beans temporarily stacked by the sapling). The fire spat donkey-high flames.

'Gotta be bigger,' said Wilbert. He retrieved two wooden bins from the marine shop.

'Gotta be higher,' said Wilbert. He dragged the last display table down the steps and rolled it onto the bonfire.

'No, no, no!' screamed Silù. He danced after Wilbert carrying an unheated pot of pigeon soup: Wilbert was bearing Silù's rickety desk down the steps towards the fire.

'All or nothing!' said Wilbert. He tossed the desk onto the pile in a fountain of sparks. 'And I'm going for "All". Every last damn thing in the shop. The king's got to see this sail.'

The angel launched string beans at Silù; they sputtered and fell short. 'Stop him, no more chances! Or you'll never get through the Kunjerab Pass. You'll never get to your charter yacht and get sailing. Wilbert, make him stop!'

'We start again,' screeched Silù. 'My idea, your funds. Eighty-twenty, me-you! Fair, fair!' He raised the pot to dump pigeon soup on the pulsing flames.

The Silk Road Chandlery

As the string beans tumbled to a halt in the dust before the bookkeeper, Wilbert's eyes riveted upon Silù. He grabbed the bookkeeper's wrist and bent it backward; in an instant, Wilbert had wrestled the soup pot from Silù's grasp and emptied it over the bookkeeper's head. Silù opened his mouth to speak, but took one look at Wilbert's face and for the first time ever, didn't say a word. He hunched, turned and shuffled back into the darkened, gutted shop, avoiding Wilbert's steaming glare.

'No soup for dinner,' said the angel.

'Nope,' said Wilbert and settled on the front steps with his angel to wait for the king.

Long after what should have been dinnertime, a pair of shiny emerald mountain bikes broke Wilbert and the angel's reverie. Two cyclists coasted round the corner, popping out of the sidestreet that led from the market place. They pulled up under the hand-painted Chandlery sign on the sapling and rifled through a guidebook. Behind the fire's sparks, far down the road into town, the dust was beginning to stir: at first a swirling puff in the distance, then larger and larger.

'You Wilbert?' asked the younger cyclist, looking up from her book. The pipe cleaner antennae attached to her khaki cap waved unevenly. 'Says here you're the last bike repair place before the Kunjerab –'

'I *was* the last place,' said Wilbert, his eyes on the dust cloud. 'Not any more. We're closed!'

The dust darkened into the heads and shoulders of tall figures swaying rhythmically toward the marine shop.

'You got any brakes left? Or . . .' She consulted her book. 'Winches?'

'Gone, everything's gone. Heading for the Pass myself tomorrow. I'm selling my masterpiece sail and finally getting out!'

Silù materialized in the doorway, looking up the street. He stood stiffly inside his flat shirt and unwrinkled underwear.

'Customers!' he gloated softly, his shoulders relaxing. 'Customers with camels. Customers with tired camels that skirted the desert of final death and still need to make it to Kashgar!'

Errol Scott

Wilbert looked up. There, approaching Wilbert's Silk Road Chandlery, in flowing robes and high atop an embroidered saddle on the first camel, was a magnificent king; behind him twisted a procession as far as the corner. All along his camel train and among his goatherds, sheep, donkeys and a dreadlocked yak, there wasn't a single yacht in sight. The king tightened his reins and paused next to the sparking fire.

'Hallo!' called the king's assistant on foot at the king's side.

'Er... hello,' said Wilbert in a small voice as he got to his feet.

The gorilla bared her fangs at the king from behind Wilbert's ear: 'No marine trailer!' she whispered.

'Welcome . . .' Wilbert looked up and down the king's entourage. 'There's . . . there's only camels!' he blurted out.

'And sheep, tired sheep!' said Silù from the doorway.

The king swayed in time with his camel and looked at Wilbert. 'We do not always find what we look for,' he said softly.

Wilbert examined some leaves at his feet that had escaped the fire; his eyes filled up watery bright. No marine trailer. No algae-covered ropes, no shiny brass fittings, no mast of any length to bear any masterpiece sail. From the last sheep's hind to the hem of the king's cloak, there wasn't even a looped ripcord that might belong to an inflatable raft. There would be no sail funds for Wilbert to go forward with and there was no way to go back. The bonfire crackled over Wilbert's heaped up inventory.

'No boat, no boat!' crowed Silù, jumping up and down and creasing the knife-pleats in his unbelievables. 'Camels are the ships of the desert! You see? We start again – equal partners, me and you, eighty-twenty!' He scurried back through the shop to the inventory shed.

The gorilla fluffed her feathers.

'I see grommets!' she said suddenly to Wilbert. Her wings began to quiver. 'Under that packing blanket, they're glinting. He's reefed his camel!'

She darted up to hover over the blanket that wrapped the last camel.

'You're last mount – it's not quite . . . hump-shaped,' said Wilbert to the king.

'It's our *sail*,' replied the king's assistant, puffing his chest.

The Silk Road Chandlery

'Been in the royal family for years. We've been, ah . . .' He glanced up at the king. 'Waiting for the right moment to use it.'

'Where there's sails, there's boats!' cried the angel.

Silù reappeared in the doorframe, his arms loaded with greasy tubes, massage mittens and nail polish. He was just in time to see the king's assistant stride to the last camel and pull back the packing blanket: the hull of a racing craft hung upside down over the camel's hump. A telescoping mast and a boom were lashed along either side of the animal who was serenely chewing its bit.

The cyclists next to Wilbert gasped; their antennae bobbed and dipped above their caps. Silù dropped his armful of tubes and polish. A little gorilla-shaped engine began to rev its wings inside Wilbert's stomach. The king, however, took no notice at all: he was admiring the magnificent sail draped from the awning of Wilbert's Silk Road Chandlery.

'That's a fine, a very fine . . . not embroidered, of course, but the curve . . . such a very full draft . . .'

'A poor substitute for your heirloom,' said Wilbert. 'But by using my sail you could protect your own. You could test it out on Lake Tianchi. As it happens, I'm headed that way.'

'Water? Lake Tianchi?' squeaked the assistant. 'Isn't that rather . . . deep? We've never been so far from the Taklamakan.'

'Not as deep as sand,' said the little gorilla. She stretched a wingtip towards the unripe figs tucked in the assistant's shirt pocket.

'My sail would need to be fine-tuned on the water by a master, of course . . .' The king nodded and then flicked his reins. 'Lake Tianchi.'

He led his camel back onto the sandy road towards the Karakoram Highway, the Hunza valley and shining, gusty Lake Tianchi. 'Sometimes,' said the king over his shoulder, 'We do not look for what we find.'

'We'll buy every boat part you've got!' said the assistant, handing Wilbert a tooled leather sack filled with paper and coins. 'Your camel will be the next one to the last. Say – your bookkeeper's looking rather green –'

'Goat lactose intolerance,' moaned Silù, swaying. 'Sharper and sharper behind the eyes!'

The angel had flapped to Silù's back and was trying, with

surprising success, to pile a fig into his ear. 'More like a case of injustice,' she hissed.

The older cyclist cleared her throat. 'Boat parts? Me too. I could do with a bike light,' she said.

'Never had any,' said Wilbert to the cyclist. He smiled as he rolled up the shimmering sail for transport. 'Got two oceanworthy kerosene signal lamps left though. Blankets, cooking pots, cutlery. And ligament ointment, I've got loads of camel ligament ointment. All yours!'

The king's assistant strapped the sail-fit-for-a-king along the boom hanging from the camel and packed Wilbert's suitcase and few things into the camel's saddle bags. Wilbert picked up the little gorilla and placed her in the dip of the camel's neck before the saddle; she flapped her wings gently to keep her balance.

'You won't make it!' shouted Silù. 'You stay here in the shop, pay rent and make money!'

The angel flapped more determinedly and rose above her seat; she launched a string bean at the bookkeeper.

'I'd rather die in the desert trying to sail than spend another minute here with you, Silù.' Wilbert drew back his fist at the same time as the gorilla and hurled his keys at the bookkeeper. 'Pack your things and get out!'

The angel's string bean merged with Wilbert's keys midair; together they hit Silù squarely between the eyes and fell to the ground in front of him. Silù knelt to sift in the sand for the keys, tearing his indescribables as he did so. He dragged himself to his feet and off to scratch at the door of the next shop, his dusty underwear flapping about his spindly legs, the empty money tin banging against his hip.

Wilbert stepped into the cupped hands of the king's assistant and climbed into the saddle behind his angel. He swivelled to look back at the Silk Road Chandlery.

The door was dark, the fire nearly exhausted. The desert sun was melting from pale lemon yellow to mandarin to red-purple in the gathering indigo darkness; it vanished beyond the desert horizon in a split second flash of green. The cyclists weaved off in the dark to their hotel, ship lights swinging from their handlebars. Over on the sapling at the kerb, the crumpled leaf

The Silk Road Chandlery

stirred; it unfurled, floated up and drifted on a breeze that wasn't there to alight on the camel rump behind Wilbert.

'Lake Tianchi,' whispered Wilbert. He dug in his heels and the camel grudgingly started off. At his side, the new bag of coins clinked. He loosened the strings to peak in.

'Not a fleet of charter boats, but enough for one very fine yacht. It's a start!'

Wilbert's camel padded forward in the wake of the king; the green eyes of his angel peeped over the arm he had curled protectively about her. On the swaying camel rump behind Wilbert, facing the point in the desert road where the snowy peaks of the Karakoram Mountains soon would appear, the crumpled leaf inhaled and stretched out its wings.

Sebastian Groes
An Interview with Iain Sinclair

An Interview with Iain Sinclair

Poet, novelist and filmmaker Iain Sinclair (Cardiff, 1943) grew up in the industrial Welsh landscape but settled in Hackney (East London) in the late sixties. Although educated as a documentary filmmaker, his 'brilliant career in cinema was over before it began'. The early work, published by Sinclair's own independent Albion Village Press, stakes out his imaginary territory: the alternative histories of (East) London(ers) that are repressed by the political and cultural mainstream. In the long poem *Lud Heat* (1975), an occult theory is constructed around five Hawksmoor churches, the British Museum and the Greenwich Observatory. The conspiratorial novel *White Chappell, Scarlet Tracings* (1987) interweaves Arthur Conan Doyle's *A Study in Scarlet* (1888) with the Jack the Ripper mythology. In the course of time his idiosyncratic visions of the city have come to supplant Peter Ackroyd's hegemony as the contemporary London writer *par excellence*.

Sinclair is the real thing: fiercely opposed to the academic petting zoo with its 'scholarly babytalk', and uncompromisingly hardcore and original in his poetics as well as politics. His more recent work shows ever bigger signs of frustration about the impossibility to stop what he sees as London's decline through 'sweetheart deals between government and private developers'. Driven by a furious yet fertile wrath, *Downriver* (1991) is a carnivalesque and apocalyptic satire on the Thatcher regime. After the mid-nineties Sinclair embarked on a triptych of nonfictional books of London walks. *Lights Out for the Territory* (1997) consists of nine secret excursions inside London, mapping out the city's forgotten writers and artists. The bestseller *London Orbital* (2002), his now infamous odyssey around the 117 mile long orbital motorway of London, is a scathing attack on New Labour's destruction of London by means of its regeneration projects. The cycle will be completed by an echo of poet John Clare's walk from an asylum in Epping Forest to his home in Werrington, *Edge of the Orison (In the Traces of John Clare's Journey out of Essex)* due out from Hamish Hamilton in September 2005.

I met Sinclair at his house in Hackney with trepidation: the author, an old school Londoner, was aware that I lived in the bourgeois north London village Crouch End, mockingly known by working-class specialists in inverted snobbery as 'Crouchant'. This would make me a butt of ridicule. However, Sinclair was courteous and patient, his spoken words baring hardly a trace of the paranoid deliriousness that characterises his written voice. Soon the conversation was on its way. Except that it was not. Upon returning home and ready to transcribe the conversation, I discovered that the tapes contained nothing but static. Sinclair, who has portrayed himself as a shaman or mystic throughout his work, was not surprised in the least. 'I'm afraid my electro-magnetic fields play up with sensitive instruments,' he would later write, half serious, half jocularly. Speedy extrapolation of extensive notes made and generous supplementations provided by the author managed to retrieve the dialogue on the death of London, heavy metal cosmology, UEA's Creative Writing programme and auditory hallucinations.

Sebastian Groes: In *Lud Heat* (1975), you displayed your dislike of the academic world and its 'scholarly babytalk'. Last year saw a conference on your work. Did this leave you feeling prematurely buried?

Iain Sinclair: The conference was all on dead work, books that were already out in the public domain. Retrievals from the Dead Letter Office. I preferred the A13 project that was going on at the old Wapping Hydraulic Pumping Station at that time. However, the location itself, the University of Greenwich, was interesting: the building which housed the conference had elements of Hawksmoor, which gave it some sentimental attraction: if, like me, you want to persist in reading London typography as a series of interconnections and erased memories. But now it had become an academic shell, a zoo with scholars running around trying to tame my work. So, yes, I was uneasy about the whole thing. On the other hand, in the contemporary climate of cultural industrialization such a conference is actually a good thing. I am glad that I have not become pre-forgotten. Silenced.

An Interview with Iain Sinclair

Groes: In the past, there have been questions about what could be called the selective politics of inclusiveness of your work. It is evident that you speak on behalf of an underclass by narrating histories of people that have been repressed or, to use your terminology, 'pre-forgotten' by the mainstream. However, academics such as Peter Brooker and reviewer Rachel Potter have accused you of excluding ethnic minorities and women from your work; Robert Sheppard also states that 'the position of women in your work is problematic. They are often reflectors of male desire.'

Sinclair: [cuts in] Why should I? I can only speak for myself. I have no obligation to speak on behalf of other people. That idea is too compulsory, extremely patronising and politically correct. I never feel that writing should be judged by what it doesn't do, it should be taken to task for what it actually does. And means to do.

Later work, such as *Dining on Stones* (2004) and my book based on John Clare's walk from Epping Forest to Werrington, gives, I hope, a more generous (if peculiar) response to the female voice, that haunting other. I worked with Rachel Lichtenstein on *Rodinsky's Room* (1999). Rachel made her quest for the mundane, human Rodinsky into a search for lost fathers, traces of her grandparents, memories of a vanished society. Another artist, equally obsessed with the Rodinsky myth, was Liat Uzyiel. Forbidden access to the decommissioned Princelet Street Synagogue, she recreated the locked room, its precise proportions, and plotted Rodinsky's movements, at every hour of the day, with a fantastic machine that scratched patterns of dust from the walls. The dust, as it fell on photographic plates, mapped an absence. The logic of this experiment, I felt, had something brave, determined – and female – about it. I also worked with Effie Paleologou during the *London Orbital* (2002) and the A13 projects. The portraits of people and the filtering of the landscape are influenced by those with whom the walk is taken. The walks with women for my work differ from those with men. Women see things differently.

Sebastian Groes

Groes: But what I wanted to ask you is whether your work is misread, given that much of it is obsessed with the disappearance of public space in relation to collective moral responsibility?

Sinclair: My work is only accidentally public. It's a response to the pressures I assume that we all feel, living in cities: wall-to-wall mendacity, civic corruption, the perversion of language. Invent a new system, a strategy for survival, or endure a system imposed on you from above. Blake's aphorism still makes sense. The notion of opposition, through writing or performance, no longer plays. I find myself invited to give talks to conferences or at City Hall. And I'm beginning to understand that if you agree to oppose, you agree. Your critique is turned and neutralized. When they give you a cheque and print your photograph in the brochure, your theoretical rant is mother's milk instead of venom.

Groes: Could you tell something about your new project, the John Clare book, *Edge of the Orison*?

Sinclair: The new book chronicles poet John Clare's walk from an Epping Forest asylum to his Northamptonshire home. *Edge of the Orison* began as a response to Clare's hallucinatory account of his walk, a walk I felt obliged to repeat, and it turned into a meditation on place, landscape, exile, the impossibility of living in town or country. Clare's Northamptonshire village has now been swallowed up by Peterborough, as part of a grotesque offroad, estate-building enterprise: the same madness that proposes the 'Thames Gateway' development as an answer to the shortage of affordable housing. When we arrived in Helpston, after a three-and-a-half day walk, we found Clare's peasant cottage offered for sale: at £475, 000.

Following up on a theme of drowning, because Clare's horizons were fixed by the Fens, and by two great rivers, we learnt about the drained Whittlesey Mere, once the largest inland sea in southern England. That such a thing could vanish and that stones, intended for Ramsey Abbey and Ely, rose up out of the peat: this was exciting. Only by travelling, at walking speed,

An Interview with Iain Sinclair

down canal and river systems, were we able to solve questions that couldn't be unpicked on land. Drowning, flying, dreaming positioned themselves as key elements in this narrative.

One myth would always fold into another. Investigating a claim, made by my wife's father, that he was related to Clare, I stumbled onto my own connection to Samuel Beckett. Visiting Alan Moore in Northampton, to find out about Clare's time in the asylum, Beckett reappeared, to become part of the sad history of James Joyce's daughter, Lucia, who died in the same hospital as Clare.

Groes: Speaking of apparitions, in the final chapter of Alan Moore's novel *Voice of the Fire* (1996), 'Phipp's Staircase', a friend, the sculptor and poet Brian Catling, and you are staging a performance in Northampton, which spirals out of control when some lunatic attacks you.

Sinclair: [cuts in] That actually happened. Moore invited us for a poetry reading and performance, and at some point this madman in the crowd pulled out a gun, started waving it around and threatening us. Shots were fired, teeth spat out on the floor of a pub. 'A normal Northampton night,' Alan Moore called it. 'A random stroll-by shooting.' *Voice of the Fire* tells the whole story. Northampton is a very strange place. And Alan has made himself its memory man – whose job is to road-test the myths and legends, to find a way forward. He thinks, after reading something by Stephen Hawking, that the gravitational field of Northampton 'mangles' information. Moore's prose is a way of de-mangling local excesses. Call it heavy metal cosmology.

Groes: In that chapter Moore describes Catling and you as 'shamanic presences', whose mysticism invokes violence. You've always refused to admit you are a shaman, or a mystic. What do you make of Moore's characterization?

Sinclair: 'Shamanic' is a misnomer. I've always seen shamanism as a metaphor for what art can do. I helped organize an event at the Goldmark Galley, in Uppingham, called 'The Shamanism of

Intent'. There was a certain amount of talk about 'sickness vocations' and willed visions as a proper response to political inertia and cultural entropy. I notice that a recent book by Anthony Mellors has a chapter called 'Shamanism and the poetics of Late Modernism: J.H. Prynne'. Mellors quotes from the Goldmark Show and states: 'It is largely taken for granted today that the "metaphor" of the poet as arcane magician affirms the revolutionary potential of the neo-romantic visionary.'

Alan Moore, unusually, has decided to go all the way: and become a practising magician. He worships a snake god, summons entities to his Northampton terraced house and prophesies the end of the world. I just use that stuff about shamanism as a metaphor, with some suspension of disbelief, some free floating irony.

Groes: *The Verbals*, Kevin Jackson's book-long interview with you, mentions that you have experienced 'auditory hallucinations', meaning that you were invaded by voices that you were able to transcribe. This happened first when you were fourteen and continued during your early adulthood. Do you still have these kinds of experiences?

Sinclair: Auditory hallucinations belonged to a particular era. They were sounds from buried scripts, trashed lives. Now such things are lost in the general acoustic landfill of London life: helicopters, sirens, screams, dogs on balconies. Hackney is itself a giant auditory hallucination. A crude Xerox of something like the LA cop show drama, *The Shield*. The speedy shamanism of late-Ellroy: slasher-killer prose composed in heavy black type. In headlines.

Groes: In Patrick Keiller's film *London* (1993), the narrator states that London is the first metropolis to have disappeared completely because its original historical centre has become aborted and faked for tourists. Your work also analyses the complicity of CCTV in making London a prison-like city.

Sinclair: The City of London is overwatched and overworked. London has become eviscerated: CCTV mediates everything through the dumb oracle of the monitor screen and the camera pole. We live in a polis of sleepwalkers: there is no dialogue. We can act, be observed, logged. But our behaviour is of no importance – until we transgress. The City of London is no longer London. It is the capital of finance only, a zone with peculiar privileges and invisible barriers. It has its own police force, but it has been emptied of meaning. The last thing it needed was Peter Ackroyd's bulky biography of London, like a big tombstone placed on top of it all.

Thames Gateway is another narrative device, a plot (hatched by New Labour, Ken Livingstone, various planners and speculative builders) to extend London beyond its physical boundaries by means of satellite development. Once again, politicians confuse the Virtual with the Actual. They fly over an empty landscape and decide that it must be exploited. They bring colour to a grey screen, invent hyperspace arcadias that can never be realised. The Millennium Dome is the prime example. The virtual colonization of the Lea Valley, for future Olympic Circuses, is a betrayal on an even grander scale The M25 replaces the Thames as a working river. London is turned inside out: the road is the highway into a devastated future, the centre is a theatre of heritage. Faked Shakespearian theatre, power station converted into art gallery, seat of local government handed over to rapacious adman, Saatchi.

Groes: These developments are part of a larger renegotiation of place in general. Deleuze and Guattari call this process 'de- and reterritorialization', by which global capitalism in a sense rewrites traditional places into bland non-spaces and gated communities. You describe many of these in *London Orbital*, such as Bluewater, one of Europe's biggest shopping centres. Could you say something about the way culture in general itself is affected by this process?

Sinclair: In the M25 film I made with Chris Petit [*London Orbital* – SG], JG Ballard tells me to 'blow up Bluewater'. He's talking about the retail city in the Kent quarry. In recent weeks, we've had footage of tanks protecting Bluewater. New Manipulators decided that a satellite shopping city is a proper target for virtual terror, or the threat of terror. We will therefore wave through new laws and abdicate old freedoms. Ikea launch a shopping fortress like a prison in Iraq. Result? Riots, clogged motorways, carnage. A town like Cheltenham, staid Regency architecture, symbol of old Empire, opens a shopping mall called 'Adorn' (like a homage to Adorno). It contains sex boutiques as well as generic merchandisers. In Amsterdam this kind of thing would be fine, it wouldn't be noticed but here it sticks out like a sore thumb. Just as art galleries are not out of place in Rotterdam, in England many cultural venues have something odd about them. Take Tate Britain, which used to be a prison, the Millbank Penitentiary. When you enter the building from the back, you can actually still see some of the cell blocks. Even now you can feel the spirit of imprisonment. Tate Modern has all the qualities of a hospital. There is something Fritz Langian about it. When I go to Holland, Rotterdam for instance, the museums have a sense of freedom about them. Locations such as Tate Modern express the odd position that culture occupies in Great Britain.

Groes: The Swiss Re building by Norman Foster, commonly known as the Gherkin, was awarded the annual Stirling RIBA Prize 2004 and this made it officially the most important building in the UK last year. It was suspiciously well received by the public as well. Do you think we should distrust its enthusiastic reception?

Sinclair: The Gherkin is part of the Virtual City imposing on old liberties, the chaos of Aldgate. Here again is the benevolent fascism of surface: all viewpoints dominated by a gigantic dildo. . . . At best, the object looks like one of the proposals by Claes Oldenburg. The nice thing about those is that they were modest enough to remain unmade. The mistake is to let vanity pitches climb off the screen. Almost all art in the city is to do with budget and being able to take a good meeting. Lord Coe and his tame celebrities waiting for their turn at the podium, with a suitable riverside backdrop. The churches of London were dominant, but they were designed to coexist with the other

An Interview with Iain Sinclair

buildings already there. The Gherkin is simply a hoarding advertising itself, or rather Norman Foster and his company. It is a building without content or interface.

Groes: But it is not only the actual building itself, but also the planners and developers who disregard the context in which they build. You have called this '[b]latant white space-ism: architects ignore the implications of where their buildings will be sited. Nothing exists beyond the frame of the idealized sketch.' This destroys London's originally medieval, messy and organic 'figure ground' – the layout of the city's streets and buildings – which is how London somehow sustains itself. Do you think the development of gated communities, such as The Imperial Wharf in Chelsea, is part of this process as well?

Sinclair: At first gated communities emerged on the periphery of London, but now they are taking over the centre of London as well. There is some sort of inversion going on of the suburbanization that John Betjeman wrote about, where you see that the centre becomes suburbanized through hideous non-development projects. The City of London now belongs to multinationals. If you walk through Oxford Street, the shops you find are taken over by global commercial monsters. As a result of the dominance of this global capital, cultural life has atrophied: you simply cannot go to the theatre anymore because the prices are too high. London has become a Fortress.

Groes: If I were to play the devil's advocate, I could point out that London's history shows that the city's development has always been characterized by a lack of government regulation. That this *laisser-faire* tradition, with its absence of heavy government intervention, has been responsible for the city's organic structure and has allowed it to survive for so long.

Sinclair: Well, the Greater London Authority had in my view a very sensible vision, which was ripped out under Thatcher. In Hackney there used to be a perfectly good swimming pool, which was demolished in order to make way for a incredibly expensive

Sebastian Groes

new one as an expression of New Labour's ideology. Like the Millennium Dome, it turned out to be a white elephant and it had to be closed soon after opening. Now Hackney is left without a swimming pool. Another public space is destroyed. London is slowly swallowed up.

Groes: At one point you say that the writers of London have divided London amongst them like feral beasts: Ballard in Shepperton, Angela Carter south of the river, John Healy walks down the Cally Road, Ackroyd celebrates Clerkenwell, Aidan Dun 'gets' King's Cross. In a way, these writers held London together by means of their writing, creating some kind of textual body which may perhaps be Frankenstein's sewn-together monster, but there was some kind of coherence to it. You yourself have increasingly sought the periphery of London, evidenced by *London Orbital*, the Hastings expedition *Dining on Stones* (2004) and now *Edge of Orison*. London appears to have fallen apart. Can writers no longer hold the capital together?

Sinclair: This was the case ten years ago. We were like gangland warriors who had staked out their territory. Mike Moorcock lived in Notting Hill and created a whole mythology around his patch. But this is not so any more. Monica Ali doesn't live in Brick Lane, and in her novel she has created a model from some place else. Zadie Smith has some grand take on the city, which has multicultural elements in it but which is basically suburbanized. Unlike Moorcock they are not creating a new mythology for the city. That is why the city is falling apart.

Writers now re-imagine other writers, often American, and are occupied with strategies of survival. London sells itself as a cultural heritage franchise. There will be many books on the place that is not Brick Lane, simply because that street no longer exists. It has lost its mystery. Only someone as persistent as Rachel Lichtenstein goes on gathering word-of-mouth stories. She visits old people and chases down the last traces. The form has developed shifts between reportage, poetry, biography, archaeology: fiction has been stripped of its privileged status. Ackroyd, for example, will publish a biography of Blake or Dickens, then a gothic novella, an improvisation on Chaucer as period crime mystery, and then a massive accumulation of post-historical tropes. New practitioners, such a Conrad Williams, might feel that the place to move is, literally, underground: back into science fiction, subterranean and subversive imaginings. A city of hungry viruses in which the author is a damaged and unreliable participant, of no special account in the telling of the tale.

Much of this has to do with speed. In the period that Gilbert and George moved to Spitalfields, it would take a long time before such a place would become 'trendy'. There would be a slow, gradual build-up. Now there is a rush to Hoxton that takes three weeks. People have such predatory, pornographic eyes when it comes to real estate. This also goes for London writing. We require smoother surfaces, sharper effects. Some contemporary writing is like copywriting for success. There is such an element of calculation and careerism. Such an effort to charm with seductive prose. Moorcockian complexity seems to belong in another century.

Groes: In an article on your work, poet Simon Perril speaks of the fires of London, such as the Great Fire of 1666 and the Blitz, as 'a symbol of visionary potential of desires for reform and the physical manifestation of their destructive failure'? I was wondering whether the Momart warehouse fire of May 2004, which destroyed a part of Charles Saatchi's collection of art by Brit artists such as Tracey Emin and the Chapman brothers, could perhaps be read as a sign of the corruption of the contemporary art culture?

Sinclair: *Lud Heat* was about a posthumous city, a London of derelict zones and dirty churches. I was looking for – and finding – the heat of history. In the white Portland stone of the Hawksmoor churches you could see the fossils coming back to life. Alan Moore thinks of fire as a cultural constant – perhaps in the play against a tradition of London fog and dirt. Heat and its contrary, damp, are part of a duality of the city. Inspiration and stupidity. Energy and lethargy.

The Momart fire was obviously a significant event.

Commentators wanted to read this as a metaphor: necessary hubris, the gods destroying junk art. Some people gloated – as they gloated over the burning, in the past, of Newgate prison or the Houses of Parliament. Some people felt the loss of memory. A lot of themes are involved in this story: the way, for example, that industrial premises in places like Hackney are now used as studios and cold stores for art. Art as investment.

Groes: Do you lament the idea that, in this era of global capitalism, the do-it-yourself spirit that you grew up with in the sixties has become virtually impossible to maintain? How has it affected the publishing industry?

Sinclair: Back in the 1960s it was still possible to publish independently. Near this room where we are now sitting I used to publish books. That had something subversive. I used to walk to Camden where you had Compendium bookshop, or take the train, so a whole landscape would be involved in the expedition. I would talk to the manager of Compendium, Mike Hart, who would inform me of the latest publications. He would also sell my own books, so there was a sense of tribal exchange going on. Now, there is the London Review of Books store in Bloomsbury, which is pleasant, but lacking in the original edge, the sense of barter and imminent collapse. The reality quotient, I feel, is less convincing. The place is strategic, subject to benevolent patronage, not quite essential.

Groes: How does this affect creative writing? In *The Guardian* you said: 'To be able to sit down and write whatever you want every day is a luxury that virtually nobody has, and maybe they shouldn't have.' In another interview you state, however, that we must 'discover new forms of writing based on Modernism. But we are not allowed to do this anymore, writing *Ulysses* for twelve years.' Does the Creative Writing faculty go against the grain of the DIY-spirit? Or can these faculties, for example the famous one at the University of East Anglia, be a safe haven for such experiments, or is there something artificial about this sitting around in an endless babble?

An Interview with Iain Sinclair

Sinclair: The true creative writing of the kind that Joyce undertook is not allowed any more. The business has become completely industrialized and commercialized. Perhaps only someone like Don DeLillo is allowed to work on a book for a very long time by his publishers. But there is poisoned money that taints everything, and it creates the need for permission of some sort. UEA obviously is complicit in the creation of this whole madness; UEA's creative writing department is responsible for producing some of the most horrendous writers around today. Although, was W.G. Sebald working in the faculty?

Groes: Yes, he was Professor of European Literature, but he was also involved in teaching creative writing and supervising creative writing students.

Sinclair: Oh. [Followed by a long silence that voices Sinclair's admiration for Sebald.] Well, writers who are truly writers have the compulsion to write everyday; they are living on the edge and do not need to enter a creative writing faculty. They will write anyway. Truly good writing has a kind of desperation to it.

Of course there still some sort of 'unofficial' creative writing classes going on. People send me their writing, and some of it is very good, but it will not be published in the contemporary climate. I am slowly assembling a book called *London: City of Disappearances* – with contributions from people like J.G. Ballard, Will Self, Marina Warner, Michael Moorcock, Rachel Lichtenstein, Alan Moore. And others, many others you wouldn't know. I'm trying to create a city of disturbed memory, stories of lost buildings, destroyed paintings, vanished people, and dispersed ghettoes. London is more absent than present. I suppose I'm coming back, as I get older and less inhibited, to those auditory hallucinations.

Groes: Are there still means for resistance to these processes?

Sinclair: You can always resist these developments. The human imagination is intensely powerful, but what you now see is that inertia is rooting itself in the human psyche. This is what

Sebastian Groes

Ballard's contemporary work is about: people are bored out of their skulls, ultimately leading to violent outbursts. There is a feeling of terror which is linked to the contemporary fear of terrorism induced by governments. Suddenly there appear fully armoured tanks at Heathrow, giving an Orwellian edge to living in London. So the nature of the game has changed. Living in London is now determined by polarization: there is a great dark underworld determined by a black market dealing in arms, drugs and prostitution. This manifests itself openly in Hackney, but sooner or later these people will arrive in Crouch End as well. I'm sure that the dealers are already buying their way into the comfort of that place.

simon@pform.co.uk

Alison Croggon
The Gilded Man
An extract
***&* Four Poems**

The real which is lost in language
— *Michel de Certeau*

And should I at your harmless innocence
Melt, as I doe, yet public reason just,
Honour and Empire with revenge enlarg'd,
By conquering this new World, compels me now
To do what else though damnd I should abhor.
Book IV Paradise Lost, John Milton

Chapter 2

I dreamt last night that I was asleep on the floor of the house in which I lived as a child. It was a very humble house, divided half for the family, and half for the beasts, who stamped and snorted at its other end as we slept; there was one wall between us. It was dark inside, and stank of cows and sheep and human fug and woodsmoke, which could not always find its way outside through the hole in the roof. We slept, my sisters and my father and I, on a kind of shelf, and were warm, cuddled up with our fleas in the steam of dung. I liked it; I knew no better. But in this dream, I was alone; I was asleep on the floor, and it was cold, and the cold woke me up. And when I woke up, I found my head was lying on a pumpkin. I sat up in surprise and looked at the pumpkin; and it looked back at me, for I noted without surprise that it had eyes. It blinked, and announced it was King Philip of Spain; it then screwed up its face and spat at me. I was so

The Gilded Man

outraged at this offensive behaviour that I hit it, and it smashed as pumpkins smash, but then I realized that it wasn't a pumpkin at all, but my little sister Angela, whose head I had broken open, and she looked up at me, the back of her skull caved in, weeping and holding out her arms, and in a panic of horror and loathing I hit her again and again, to rid myself of her piteous expression, and then I woke up with her warm blood all over my face. I sat up, trying to wipe it out of my eyes with my hands, but it wouldn't stop dripping, and I realized I must be bleeding myself, and so lifted the cloth of my bed to stanch the wound, and the top of my skull fell into my hands, cut as cleanly as if it had been sliced with a razor. I instantly felt very foolish; what I must look like with the top of my head missing! and I looked around the room for a hat to hide it, but I couldn't see properly, and in any case I knew it was useless, and that there was no hat in the room. But still I kept looking, with a kind of heavy hopelessness. And then I woke up properly, the sweat running down my face so that for a second I thought I was still back in my dream.

    I cannot reconcile myself to the uselessness of my existence. I abhor this task of writing; I look at the sheets which await me with disgust and hatred. With what ignorant joy I received the gift of literacy! For days on end I sit in this room, staring out of the grimy opaque window, and turn my back on the paper. I do! As if the paper were a person who would take offence, and flounce out in insult. It never does; when I am bored with staring at the wall, or studying the cobwebs, it is always there, just as it was before I turned my back. I fancy it looks at me with reproach. I fancy it is already soured, like a disillusioned mistress, by my procrastinations; how I will do anything, anything, except tell this story I have to tell. It knows all my excuses, how well it knows them! I am convinced it sniggers behind my back, when I am pretending it's not there; I am certain it does. It doesn't care, it's only paper, it can wait as long as it likes. It knows I will return, in the end, to the table, and dip the quill in the inkbottle, and make another mark. It knows that with the contemptuous certainty of triumph. For I have nothing else to do.

    How miserable this death is.

Alison Croggon

I have made a far from exhaustive list of the requirements for the expedition, led by Governor Ursua, to sail the Marañon River and find the Gilded Man of the Omaguas in the fabulous City of Manoa, where rivers ran over sands of gold and the very paving stones shone brighter than the sun herself. There had to be powder, arms, munitions, horses and cattle, rope and ship's stores, and of course the ships themselves, of which more later: anchors, nails, cookware, horseshoes, provision, provision and more provision for both beasts and men, plus the ornament necessary to sustain men of gentle and noble birth in such savage circumstance – robes of silk and velvet, gold chains, marks of office and such fol-de-rols: and a Bible, and the golden chalices and holy instruments of Mass. Can you, o transcendent reader of these my words, imagine the qualities required to assemble these things in such a place as Lima? For if you wish to purchase a gross of nails, you might wander down to the hardware supermarket, where you will be able to buy a dizzying variety of such things, from tiny blueblack thumb tacks to those grey nails with aluminium hats for hammering into corrugated iron, to four inch steel rods with small, discreet heads and slim long bodies, not to mention every variety in between; and if you wish to buy food, you need merely visit the supermarket, where there will be oranges from Israel and Japanese pumpkins from North Queensland and Arabian dates and Indonesian bok choy and lemongrass and saffron and almonds from the Indies and lettuces packed in ice and flown from the gardens of Werribee, all propagated with or without genetic modifications; such plenty at the mere flicker of your hand over a keyboard, the mere flourish of a signature on a small piece of plastic. For Governor Ursua, you must understand, the situation was somewhat different, and nails most assuredly did not grow on trees, although the ships he built to navigate the melancholy waters of the New World were hewed out of the virgin forest itself. What foresight, cunning, thrift and brutality, what powers of organization and improvisation and diplomacy (for we must remember that the putative Governor Ursua was much loved), were required to gather together such an inventory! However, I thought writing such a list, incomplete as it is, might sharpen my mind to the task

The Gilded Man

at hand, because I seem unable to write things down in the right order. No doubt it is my lack of education, which has not equipped me for the finer things. Or perhaps being dead has muddled my intellect; perhaps my brain, perhaps all of me, is softly decomposing without my knowledge, although I seem whole enough to me (but how is it that I do not eat? or shit? though, it is true, I breathe, I breathe through my nose).

A nose is a brave literary instrument, which it might be instructive to deconstruct, had I the time or the inclination. I have neither, and will refer You, God of my Penance, to certain Russians, certain Englishmen, certain even of the Classics. The suffering that has been caused by noses! The agonies of sensibility which have been brought to bear on this most protuberant of our facial features! The histories which have been shaped or warped by this worthless bit of gristle and skin, the Cleopatras, the Caesars, I implore you, can human expression cover it? No, I say, and so shall pass over it in silence. Think of the perorations of ink thus spent, the forests felled! And is any of it sufficient, I ask, to explain the mystery, the ineluctable nature, the true significance of a nose? Of course not. By a nose one might win an Empire or lose the meaning of life. Suffice it to say with my customary brevity that my nose is one of the few prides of my life: it sticks out of my face at a preferred angle, which belies my antecedents with a certain style, nay, nobility. I have often stared, struck, in the mirror, examining how its aquiline shape throws a most, I might say, aristocratic shadow across my lips. I have taken care to protect my nose, since by virtue of this organ alone I have been able to establish a certain moral authority over other men, men, it must be confessed, who boast none of the accoutrements of authority at all and so be it must be allowed may be cowed by a nose alone. Have they a single display otherwise, a nose will not suffice, but without, a nose is all: and so the cruellest blow on such as I is a blow which breaks my nose. It has happened, I confess, but I have so craftily and with such anxious vanity reshaped the septum, reckoning nothing of my pain, that still it shows not too badly for the life it has led. Or I think it does. There is no mirror here for me to cogitate on how my nose survived my death, and so I am forced to feel it with my fingers

Alison Croggon

(it feels as if it remains unscathed) and to checking my visible members, which all look as I recall them last. My vanity must thus exist alas! as everything else, only within my memory: I visualize myself before a mirror, and there admire the memory of my nose, as I did whenever a mirror was available, or even a still water in a bucket. I tried at the window, but it is so smudged and bleared there is no reflection possible, and in any case to reach it I had to stand on the table, which rocked and creaked beneath my feet in an alarming fashion. In my life I was often ridiculed for my obsession, but to every man belongs a few things which are beyond ridicule, which may even be said to be sacred, and with which he will persist in the face of all the world's disopprobrium and laughter, and withal, if he does not, he is not a man.

But what of my story? It seems to me that I will never get out of here if I do not begin it: but alas, I am led astray by – of all things! – my nose. So I have been led all my life. And now it seems, all my death. Existence is cruel. If I had truly deserved my nose, if I had been, after all, the scion of a wealthy family, if I had had the wherewithal by which I might have afforded virtue, which comes in a rich coin, and so is beyond the means of many of us – if I had had, in short, the money to back up my instinct for the aristocratic – it may be that I would have led an entirely blameless and perhaps even a model life. I might for example have donated to monasteries, and given alms to the poor, and alleviated by my humble example the suffering which lies all around us, with a coin here, a coin there, housing the beggars at my table, bringing the poor downtrodden eyes up to the beneficence of God, in the pathos of their awed gratitude. But instead I was born with only a rag to call my own, and a snotrag it was too, o my interlocutor, and never washed at that: and given that, how could I have made decisions other than the ones I made? For it was a constant comment that my nose was a thing apart, a sublime and extraordinary organ: and if it hadn't been for my nose, I might not have sought to better my miserable situation, I might have been herding goats at this moment, breathing in the innocent mountain air and not giving a fig for golden ingots or dreams of Imperial glory. For it was these visions boiling in my veins, this poison set there, heated into madness by

The Gilded Man

the Gilded Man, which has led me here: and that evil desire, I confess here and now, was entirely due to my nose. An accident of birth and fate! On so little, on such a minuscule flange of flesh, on such an insignificant seeming tissue, pregnant with inauspicious omen despite its meagre materiality, did my fate depend; and so I throw myself at Thy mercy, saying now: if God had not given me such a nose, such a temptation, then I might have been a good, honest and gentle man, instead of the poor sinner I now am.

Aguirre's nose rivalled mine in its imperious sweep, but I liked to think that in that area, at least, I held my own. His could be expressive of a certain demonic flair, but equally, when his eyes were uncandled by lusts, could appear insignificant. Don Ursua's nose was I thought a common proboscis, seeking not the heavens even if it were not base and eschewed the forests of blackheads and pimply extrusions and warts and efflorescences of hair which decorated most of the company. But Doña Inez possessed (and I say this humbly, with an anguish mitigated only by her sex) the most shapely and exquisite nose I have ever seen – as might have been imagined by the great sculptor himself in a moment of inspiration – delicately lined from between her black brows to where her nostrils flared out in two perfect curves, two miniature ivory premonitions of her white breasts, expressively disdainful and passionate, but with just enough – just enough of a suggestion of flesh to give her commanding austerity (which she could assume at will) a leavening hint of charm; nay, a whiff of the cunt, which softened with its innocent lubricity the sternest of her thorns. Never, in a lifetime of connoisseurship of noses, have I seen an example so fine, so indicative of at once a fine and assertive consciousness and yet also an unbridled and maybe even anarchic sensuality. And just as my fate was led by my nose, so I believe Doña Inez's was moulded by hers; and she paid terribly for it.

How hard it is to determine the beginning of anything! Is it in the seed of our father, which grows into the little homunculus inside the forebearing womb of our mother (may her name never be smirched) that first our destiny is written? Is it written inscrutably in the Book of God, marked there by the stern Angel of Records? Was I born to my destiny, or did I there lead myself,

Alison Croggon

blindly navigating crossroads which possessed a significance of which, at the time, I was wholly ignorant? And my poor narration seems to be taking as long to launch as the most humble raft of Don Ursua's expedition for the El Dorado of the Omaguas: for in truth, it was more than twenty months before the first assemblage of the expedition and its inauspicious embarkation onto the waters of the Marañon River in a series of leaky ships hammered and warped out of ill-cured wood, on that seventeenth day of September (although some record it as the sixteenth, and others say it was even in October, I remember especially that it was the seventeenth) when the boats slid into the Ribera de Mayo, tributary of the Huallaga, one vein in the vast and mysterious network of the mighty Marañon.

There was much disputation on the bank, as I remember: for of the three hundred horse, the ships could with safety take but forty, and many of the cattle also had to be left behind, all to fend for themselves. A Conquistador was most reluctant to part with his horse; apart from being valuable animals, a man with a horse could carry much more treasure than one mountless, even given the availability of slaves; and moreover, he could make a quick exit from scenes of trouble, if circumstance required. Don Ursua, passing an aristocratic hand over his brow with an affected gesture of ennui, closed the quarrel by choosing the horses of the forty most highly ranked men and bullying the rest. The horses were led onto the great rafts with some difficulty, snorting and kicking, and the sedans of the women were boarded onto the ships, with their slaves and accompaniments, and the trembling Antilleans and the three hundred noblemen, villains all for all their nobility, and then, without even a ceremonial flourish, this strange and motley fleet began its perilous quest for gold and glory. And a silence fell over all the company as the boats were pushed out into the faster currents in the middle of the vast brown river, and for a short time all that could be heard was the slap and volley of the water and, far away it now seemed, the secret insect buzzing of the jungle, punctuated now and then by the inhuman scream of a bird or a monkey.

And oblivious to this picturesque scene, King Philip of Spain lounged in his silken sheets, signalling to his personal attendants

The Gilded Man

to dance attendance. I suppose. It occurs to me that I have no idea what a King does in his private time, in the seclusion of his chambers; I have no doubt he shits and pisses, being but a man for all the godlike splendour which attends his public appearances. He bears the nimbus of a god, most truly God's representative on Earth in all his temporal glory, and like God is removed from the heavy toil and sweat which accompanies those whose blood is fated to run in humbler furrows. His absence is truly miraculous, for it is also the most Real, untrammelled, sublimely aware and unaware: beneath his lordly feet toil the dumb workers of the dumb earth, and dumbly they offer up its riches. But unlikewise, I have no idea who They are who, removed into their stratospheric realms of power, send 1500 billion American dollars of currency transactions through the ether every day. Do They, likewise, piss and shit? A single, barely perceptible gesture of their little finger, and one village is burned to the ground, another is subjected to the travails of progress, a third is sold the necessary arms to subjugate a fourth. So the King sits, in his realm most Real, while from his unimaginably fleshly fingers stretch little cobwebs, ever more and more and more attenuated and more complex, which become millions nay billions of actions and transactions. The present King is more Divine, being invisible, and therefore even more Real than he has ever been. He moves with the inevitability of Nature herself. He may even be God, since he does not exist and yet is the source of all power, extra-territorial and ubiquitous. He has conquered geography and has swallowed nature. But surely even He – whoever He is – pisses and shits, even if his sheets are made of pure titanium. Only I, of all living things, do not piss and shit. But I, I believe, am not alive . . . although I am told the borders between the living and the not living are becoming more and more blurred, and consequently the soul of man a disputed territory, a contested region of the borderline between life and death. Therefore I may be absolutely modern, especially in my obsolescence. (Who tells me? I dream these things, they flicker on the humble walls of my mind, this poorly lit cave in which I crouch, wondering what is real and what is not real: for if I am real, then what is my purpose? and if I am not real, what is the agency of my thought? These things puzzle me to the point of anguish).

Alison Croggon

Whatever his provenance, King Philip of Spain is as responsible for our actions as is the Don Ursua; his ultimate authority lies behind each action of ours, in protest, lament, obedience or rebellion; his Divine ordering, second only to the Pope and then to God Himself, is without question. Only a certain answer to the question of his digestive functions could bring the stink of common humanity about his gleaming shoulders (for how can they not gleam in our dark minds, so uncertain after all that we are real): and who should have the courage to ask him? And although I assume that he does, *I cannot be sure*. He may well be made of stuff other than us. I have never seen him. Those who have, or who have heard from those who have, say he is a man: but he is a man who wields absolute power, and how can a man who wields absolute power be wholly a man? Nevertheless, man or divine flesh, I pondered King Philip of Spain, as the boats pushed slowly into the river. He knew or cared nothing of us: of this I was as certain as I could be of anything. He would continue to know or care nothing until we brought back the gold of El Dorado; then perhaps we would be permitted a little of his reality, his recognition, his authority, his mortal Divinity. Until such time as that, we were condemned to toil in the shadows, mere reflections of men, insect-flesh uneasily condemned to its unillumined fate. And for this permit, this entry, at last, into the Kingdom of the Real, we were prepared to gamble everything – for what is life if it is but a phantasmagoria of hope, the possibility of fire, but never the flame itself?

And here you might ask: among these silences, these silences of the silent flesh of which I am but a single unit, what of those others? What of the writings which are burned by the obedient priests? What of those glances, so full of meaning, which vanish into the temporal abyss? What of the gestures which flash once and are no more? What of the lost languages? For they are so full of words, but they are not the words of our civilization, my civilization, they inhabit the unreal although they constitute the real. Without the arms which impotently resist rape, without the woman who covers her child's eyes so he will not see his murderer, without the labour of stick limbs in the infernos of the gold mines, without the despairing eyes of a man stricken and

The Gilded Man

condemned to death by the smallpox, without the abject fear of the villagers shrinking before the conquistadores, without the scream of an old woman mauled by the mastiffs, without the shame of a nobleman stripped of his privilege, without the self-mutilation of a woman who would be a saint, without the bruises on the face of a good wife, without the millions trembling before the hellpit, power would be nothing: nay, without these, the Real would be divested of itself, would be of as little significance as the smallest blade of grass. All its gold would *mean nothing*.

Picture to yourself, said a wise man, *the slow death of a tortured child*: and then ponder the guilt of God. And should He not feel guilt, the author of Me?

To which I say: the King feels no more guilt at the suffering of his subjects than does a housewife who pours boiling water into a nest of ants. For the suffering is not Real. And since He garnishees all the Real into his own person, this is indisputably so. My wretched existence, if it can be called that, proves it.

But I am getting lost again.

I am the Author of Fate. The Architect of Soul. The Narrator of Destiny. The Shaper of Gods. The Apotheosis of History. I see at last the alchemical reversal of God into the image of Man. How much I fear the truth of what is self-determined, how much I shudder at the thought that this is all my own inscribing, mine and other men. Who is to argue against this suspicion, in the foetid circumscription of his own miserable ego? For of course it cannot be true. But who is to prove otherwise? All of history laboured through long aeons to produce – me.

But a sense of comedy strangely eludes me. All I can perceive is the tragedy of the absurd. I weep, but no tears run down my face. I retch, but can make no bile. I laugh, but my laughter is forced and vacant. I would like to kill myself, but I am already dead. Perhaps I really am discomposing.

I mean, decomposing.

Alison Croggon

BEASTS

The beasts are retreating. They are sliding
into the dusk, into the supple light of vanishing trees,
into the glue of dreams. All their strangeness
wavers behind wire, between the four sides of a screen,
odourless and deathless. The beasts stare out of
bleached pages, enclosed at last, and the zoos
are silent, except when parrots and keepers
conduct their weird orchestrations.
Panic flicks in those slotted eyes but the sadness
is only ours. Police hunt corpses in rubbish dumps,
a pregnant mother and child. Beneath the surface,
submarine cries burst the ears of whales.
Coral is leached to stone by the stripped sunlight
and houses crouch by the shore, awaiting the wave
prophets see in the distance. In forests
that glow at night, there are boars and wolves
whose futures mutate daily. There is much that is unknown
as always and even more that now will never
be understood. The cedar forests of Lebanon
are tinder dry and bears starve on the wet tundra.
In the depths of night there may be a phone call
we dare not answer or a cry in the street
which makes the hair rise on the back of our necks.
They will not come back, something is happening
at the edge of our eyes, behind the reflections,
and billboards shout in the silence, delivering words
that in a more innocent age we thought were ours.

Bread

Whatever drags downward, the heart hampers:
        hands softer than dough
may leaven massy weights, o delicate
              knucklings of love,

those confusing perfumes, wafers taken
        out of the flesh-hot ovens
to be laid on muteness, on whatever starves
        in crowds of noise

or between walls neither silent nor friendly
        where restless shadows
take refuge from themselves, wherever
        no rains fall,

there may the tongue flood and flower:
        harsh the stone that cracks
the seed, harsh the fire, harsher still the heart's
        voiceless need.

Alison Croggon

Goodnight, sweet prince . . .

Such possessions as gore me pontificate from corners.
I am no longer solid but a speech of butterflies.
How it spills, when all is said and done:
It is hard to see virtue in the cold matter
Staining the floor – frills, cups, leaves, arquebuses,
Bile – the gross litters of meaning – the new king
Knitting up this mess in his brainless sinews,
Mere presence the answer to everything, the golden
Halo of a new dawn impressing all the peasants.

Untitled

the bees have declared an amnesty
their dances are only lyrical effusions

and why are apricots so illiterate?
yet they diffuse their promiscuous perfumes
sliming the earth with rot

one has always mistrusted the language of cats
and their devotion to hygiene

so many things slide and tumble
churches flounder in tides of mud
shoes dissolve in a week

and why do scissors keep disappearing?
if you ask nature for absolution
it senselessly posts you flowers and blood

and fronds uncurl to tinier fronds and so on
which seem meticulous synonyms for murder

like a froth of hands on metallic surfaces
making and unmaking
and underneath the mindless carnivorous ocean

Michael Holroyd
A Family Affair

Recently, when I was being interviewed about the 'Gwen John and Augustus John' exhibition at the Tate Britain, I was asked who had 'won', the sister or the brother. I suggested that it was not quite like a football match or the Olympics, but had there been such a straightforward contest Augustus would undoubtedly have backed Gwen – he was always her champion during her lifetime and after her death. But this did not satisfy my interviewer. Was it not significant, she persisted, that Gwen's name preceded Augustus's as the title of the exhibition catalogue and on the posters? Certainly, I replied, it was significant in so far as it signified that Gwen was older than her brother and therefore came first. I could tell, however, that this was not the answer she had wanted.

Reading their letters while writing a biography of Augustus John, I had found nothing that showed a pattern of sibling rivalry between them – or indeed between their little known brother and sister, Thornton and Winifred John. What I did discover was a common grief over their mother's death while they were children, a grief which manifested itself as an enduring dislike of their prodigiously long-lived father. They had a common enemy. Edwin John's sombre presence threw a shadow over their early lives in Wales from which they were all determined to escape. Thornton went off to Canada, Winifred left for the United States, Gwen lived in France and Augustus in England. It was as if they were all anxious never to put the others in a position similar to the one in which their father had placed them. The four of them found their own undisputed territories from which

A Family Affair

they maintained good relations with one another all their lives.

While they were still students together at the Slade School of Fine Art in London, Gwen sometimes found her brother's presence distracting. But that was not exclusively a family matter. Another Slade student, the artist and writer Wyndham Lewis, records feeling exactly the same. 'Near John I can never paint,' he wrote to his mother, 'since his artistic personality is too strong'.

According to Augustus himself, he and Gwen were 'not opposites but much the same really, but we took a different attitude'. Both of them loved the same woman, the mysterious 'Dorelia', and their different attitudes may be seen in their portraits of her: Gwen's intimate and moving, Augustus's idealistic and romantic. But remarkably there appears to have been no jealousy. 'Gus loves you in a much more noble way than you may think,' Gwen wrote to Dorelia. 'You are necessary for his development . . . I love you so much that if I never saw you again and knew you were happy I should be happy too.'

It was easier for Gwen to guide Dorelia back to her brother because by then she was in love with the French sculptor Rodin. Some of her letters to Rodin, seeking to elicit his sympathy, tell of disturbing dreams about her brother – and it is a curious coincidence that these two men in her life should have the same first name: Augustus and Auguste.

Of my biographical subjects, Bernard Shaw would seem to have most reason to fall victim to sibling rivalry. He loved his mother who appeared indifferent to him, much preferring her daughter Lucy. On her twenty-first wedding anniversary, she took the boat across from Ireland to England following a Svengali-like singing teacher to London and taking Lucy with her. But she left her teenage son with his unemployed, alcoholic father in Dublin and never returned.

Emerging from a lonely and miserable adolescence, Shaw was to become a born again Shavian, the phenomenal parentless GBS. This famous public figure, the very author of himself, appeared to be immune to the pain of loving but developed a weakness for strong, sober, fully-employed political men of action. Towards his sister Lucy, he maintained a steady feeling of disdain, while her attitude to him was one of mocking disbelief. All in all, he reasoned, it was an admirable arrangement, preserving a healthy sibling relationship based on an instinct planted deep in human nature to guard against incest.

My third bearded biographical subject, Lytton Strachey, the eleventh of thirteen children, was brought up in a house teeming with women. His brothers were often abroad and, longing for the time when he too could enter their adventurous masculine worlds, he kept a map on which he charted their travels.

Lytton was regarded as the most brilliant child of this large bustling family. But then, in his eighth year, his world changed. His father was seventy and his mother forty-seven when his younger brother James was born. James was an *enfant miracle*, his mother's special child, 'my loveling, my darling bird' she called him. It was then that Lytton began to develop a sequence of illnesses that may have been occasioned by a need to regain his mother's loving attention.

Both Lytton and James Strachey were homosexual. But there is little evidence of rivalry in their adult lives. James, who became the authorized translator of Sigmund Freud's works, venerated his brother who, he believed, by infiltrating libertarian beliefs through his biographies and providing them with subversive subtexts, did far more than the public realized to promote sexual egalitarianism.

The John, Shaw and Strachey families would all appear to provide rich backgrounds for sibling rivalry. But in no obvious or direct sense can it be said to have developed into their adult lives. In a society, however, that promotes competition as the most efficient means of co-operation, it is not surprising perhaps that such rivalry has become a popular concept – indeed one of the clichés of our times.

Of course it does exist. And it prospers where parents, barraged by alarming statistics and living in a culture of grades, marks and scores, urge their children to perform against each other, ironically in the interests of their security.

But then I see all this from the point of view of a single child, brought up by grandparents, longing for the company of other children and harbouring sentimental notions of sisters and brothers. I am not encumbered with a university degree yet I

A Family Affair

have been in competition all my life, my worst self perpetually struggling against my better self in a contest that provides an enigmatic spectacle for others.

José Luis de Juan
This Breathing World
Extract from a novel translated by Martin Schifino & Selina Packard

We know that venturing into the Argiletum does not make for a calm or pleasant walk, especially from the sixth hour until sunset. Who can count the number of paces that separate, say, the Forum from the main perfumers' street, the Vicus Unguentarius? Numerous hawkers force you to stop, make awkward detours, or retrace your steps to negotiate the teeming crowd. Some of these sell straw, or barter it for broken glass; others peddle the most unlikely trinkets or resell old shoes; still others offer *popinae* or hot food, as well as salted or cold meats. Those who sell beancakes are besieged at lunchtime, as are the *libelliones*, who offer old books, much sought after at dusk by readers who devour them overnight, intoxicated by the greasy, smoky fumes from their oil lamps, and who try to sell or exchange them for others the following day. The needy ply their dangerous and desperate trades; the poor propagate like ants. Improvising poets, sword-swallowers, and snake charmers share the street with quacks and procurers.

As we already know, at one end of the Argiletum and the Subura, along the slopes of the Esquilian, we can find most of the the *officinae*, or papyrus workshops. They work to produce the media for three different kinds of writing: the finest or *hieratic*; the regular or *Augusta*, and the *emporeutic*, used on packaging. Let's note, for those who may find it unfamiliar, that a *liber* is made up of twenty pages at most, glued together along the thickest side and rolled up. On each page, the writing is done in two columns, a somewhat difficult task as one must either keep the book rolled or let the sheets fall to the floor, and risk spoiling the papyrus.

This Breathing World

Every householder used to own slaves who would copy out books for his private library, but in recent times the biblipoli have monopolized the business. It is only they who have large numbers of dedicated *libraii* at their disposal, as well as scribes who take letters from dictation. The important booksellers from the Argiletum arrange for a popular work to be dictated to many amanuenses – sometimes ten or fifteen of them – at the same time. Publishers such as Pomponius Aticus, the brothers Sosii, Tryphon, or Atrectus himself – who initiated the practice of advertising new titles on the columns of the Argiletum – employ a high quality ink of great viscosity. This makes corrections problematic, and water and sponge have to be used. Even more problematic is to re-copy a page, given the scarcity of papyrus since Egypt's veto on its export, which in turn has made good sheepskin parchment hard to come by.

The written word has great value amongst us, and any excuse to take up the quill is a good one: what one says vanishes into the air, but words wrought in ink are of such importance in Rome that, in some cases, forgery can be considered as serious as the murder of a free man. In the past, when influential gentlemen could have slaves who did nothing but write all day, those slaves would never knowingly have dared make a mistake. Yet when a scribe is recording words for a stranger – for a potential reader who is not his master – certain liberties or sabotages seem possible for him, and also for the lector.

We know that reading has always been a pleasure cultivated by even the most devout sensualists. Any educated person wants to own a copy of a text, and at times, demand is so high that individual copies are not checked against the originals; at others, each amanuensis revises his writings as the text is dictated a second time by the lector, instead of exchanging copies as usual with the other amanuenses, supervised by one of the bibliopoli's foremen. How many times do the clients receive texts they take to be identical, to be copies of a particular book, but, in fact, are not? Perhaps they discuss the text at the baths, or perhaps they recite a few verses from memory – a skill that was in vogue in Cicero's lifetime, but later, during the reign of Tiberias, was considered affected, and now . . .

José Luis de Juan

Only few know of this, but it has come to the attention of wealthy aristocrats who have one library in the city and one in the country. They start learning a few epigrams in town and continue at their holiday villa, or perhaps, as is more common in the summer, start memorizing some farce or moral speech by the sea, and finish it back in the city. In the process they discover significant deviations between texts in each library. There's little cause for alarm, but the proliferation of public libraries, an activity fostered by the expansion of the Empire, may have turned this problem into a plague. Who would suspect that the very seat of the censors themselves, our own Atrium Libertatis, whose magnificence has been so exalted, and which contains busts of all the greatest authors, has scrolls stored on its shelves which are filled with falsifications and sabotages, perhaps works substantially different from those written by their original authors?

Let's imagine what may have happened if the imitative powers of the copyists had already taken hold. Let's imagine that in fact the contagion dates back to old times and that forgeries have been multiplying as each of the great libraries opened: in the library on the Palatine licensed by Augustus; the Domus Tiberianae patronized by Tiberius; in the one founded by Vespasian; or in the wealthy Ulpia Library, which Trajan built for his forum; and so on until the number of public libraries in Rome reached twenty-eight. How many works, altered, improved upon perhaps, but more likely damaged beyond repair by the copyists, do we attribute today to immortal authors? And what can we say of those we don't hesitate to name *ventriloquus,* whose inner voice expresses itself in false writing and may come to transform itself, thanks to the skill of its imitative art, into that of a poet?

There's little cause for alarm, but perhaps we should arm ourselves with a lamp, like Diogenes, and go from one end of the Argiletum and the Subara to the other, to unmask these *ventriloquui* who adulterate our words.

'Is it true that you have speared two men?'

Mazuf gazes blankly at Cafon's accounts book, lost in its fantastical figures. He looks terrible, as if he hadn't slept or eaten in weeks. His feet, half wrapped in filthy, ruined *calzei,* are

This Breathing World

covered in blisters from walking all the paved streets in Rome.

'It isn't, Cafon,' the Syrian amanuensis replies at last, half-heartedly. 'Idle gossip. Slanders.'

'Why are they saying it, then?'

'Oh, you know, rivalries, quarrels in the paederasts' quarter. It's not a big deal.'

'By Polux, Mazuf, it is to me!' Cafon bangs on the table. 'You could get me into real trouble, you know. And just when everything's ready for the opening of the new workshop. What am I going to do with my new Greek scribes, who cost me an arm and a leg, if you get caught? I haven't got another lector to read to them! It would be the end of me!'

'Don't get upset, Cafon. Please.'

Mazuf looks at him almost tenderly; he knows he owes him a lot and will come to owe him even more.

'There's no danger,' he says in his deep and persuasive voice. 'Has anyone found these bodies I supposedly killed with my spear? No, because they don't exist. No one's been killed. The rumours are being spread by a bunch of liars. Have you seen any accusations brought against me?'

'It's true, I'll give you that – there are no charges. Maybe there never will be, nothing formal anyway. But that's not the point, Mazuf. The problem is that those who used to speak enviously of your sexual exploits now go around saying you're a murderer. You know what they say: "Give a dog a bad name . . ."'

'But we don't have to listen to what they say,' Mazuf urges. 'We can't lose sleep over this, we just have to tackle it head-on. After all, actions speak louder than words.'

'What do you mean, actions? What are you talking about, you fool?'

'Everyone in the Argiletum knows of your plans to open a new workshop. Your son has decided to tell anyone willing to listen that I, a foreign slave, will become a lector like him. He's furious, and he doesn't care who knows it. He drinks too much, but that's neither here nor there. Anyway, suppose you bow to these rumours, and keep me in my present position, or try and sell me off, even though no one would give you anything for me now – you'd only be confirming everyone's suspicions, and this would affect your business. On the other hand, if you turn a deaf ear to all the gossip and carry on as planned – if you send me, as you said you might, to take Rhetoric lessons with Pelagius, if you place me at the head of the new group of scribes without further ado – then all those filthy accusations will disappear like the fog in the Argiletum at sunrise.'

The Campus Martius was freezing in the mornings. Fires and braziers proliferated along the Argiletum, and clothes of the thickest wool were brought out of storage. Along the Subara, the leafless banana trees began to shed those yellow balls freighted with dust that irritate the eyes. Only the cypresses on the Esquilian and the Capitol stood watch over the temples and the government buildings.

When everything in his life seemed to have gone into hibernation, and this feeling was embodied in the bitterness of the Roman winter, Mazuf rebuilt his strength from within. He would never be the same again: the spear he had driven into two bodies had first gone straight through his own heart; Mazuf had murdered his own innocence. No more lovers: giving up love for ever would henceforth be his badge of honour. From now on he was going to take his skills as a *ventriloquus* seriously.

Rhetoric became a delight with Pelagius. Pelagius was like him.

'True rhetoric is imitative, Mazuf,' he told him. 'It comes from within, from the heart, often in spite of ourselves. In time, the voice, or voices, that you have in your belly will become, if you're lucky, a more essential part of your life than even your dreams or deepest desires.'

Pelagius introduced him to his secrets; he'd never had a pupil like Mazuf. He seemed to intuit everything, having already worked out this or that rhetorical problem, this or that grammatical principle. Latin was not Mazuf's mother tongue, but he had embraced her as if she was a young mother who had offered her breasts to nourish the growth of his voice, the foundations of his speech. As for Greek, it had spread through Italy since the time of Hannibal. It had spread, too, through all levels of society, and even had a certain prestige amongst slaves,

This Breathing World

as many popular plays were either wholly or partly in Greek. Truly, Greek customs had penetrated every corner of Rome. Speeches in Greek were common, and Cato himself found it necessary to chastise a senator for having a Greek recitative sung at a banquet.

Nevertheless, the popularity that Greek enjoyed during certain eras brought about a lively interest in Latin: after all, they were neighbouring languages. The teaching of Latin had reached freedmen and slaves, foreigners and Greeks themselves, and the teaching methods, similar to those used by Pelagius, Athenian in origin, were taken from the Hellenes. The most learned were aware that the method was effective but lacked solid foundations on which to establish itself. It was possible to learn to speak and write Latin well enough from the Twelve Tables, but much more was needed to civilize the tongue of Latium: a national literature, still young in Rome, had yet to grow.

But we speak of other times. Now literature flourishes even as a large part of it withers rapidly away. And as much as Pelagius loves to write Greek, he is a master of Latin rhetoric. Mazuf asks to be taught his master's beautiful language. A *ventriloquus* must be a polyglot, must always be learning new tongues.

'What do you think of our comic writers – the famous ones, I mean?' Mazuf asked him one day.

'In moral or in aesthetic terms?'

'Both.'

'Let me start with the latter, then. I believe that, in Roman comedy, characters have never been well drawn, nor scenes well grounded in reality. The Romans pale beside their Hellenic models: they lack vigour, and characters and situations seem to appear randomly, as if shuffled like a pack of cards. I am not saying that no good comic writers have appeared; I am saying that our poets are better than our playwrights. Some beautiful lines come to mind, for instance, from Livius's *Tarentilla*: "To one, she nods, at another she winks/one she caresses, another embraces."'

'You choose an unforgettable poem, Pelagius.'

'As for the moral dimension,' Pelagius continues, 'I'm afraid I'll have to be quite harsh about Romans writers, perhaps harsher than I was about their staging. They have tried to reproduce foreign themes which are quite alien to them: moral indifference and public corruption. But the most disgusting immorality penetrates everywhere: the language is cynical, the feelings obscene, love has been prostituted. These imitators have done their best to advocate Greek depravity in the midst of Rome's increasing corruption. As Plautus puts it in *The Captives*, morality, that *rara avis*, has become nothing better than a more effective way of "deceiving and seducing the innocent".'

'Perhaps we should turn to tragedy, then,' said Mazuf.

Pelagius grew sombre. He disliked Roman comedy, but tragedy! Roman blood seemed thicker and more persistent than Greek: prosaic and real. And seen on stage, the results could be unwatchable. 'No, by Pallas! Greece loves heroism, courage, self-sacrifice. But Rome is only happy with rivers of blood. Have you ever come across Athenians who enjoy watching men torn to pieces by lions?'

'Yet in the scenes of a tragedy, Pelagius,' Mazuf objected, 'we learn about the true meaning of life.'

'Tragedy is about death, or rather the causes of death. I'm not interested in it.'

simon@pform.co.uk

Sarah Gooderson
Writing A Tale

'As a little girl I was angry with Hans Christian Andersen for making me suffer. I thought he was pushing my mind around. In fact he was turning me into a writer'.
– A. S. Byatt
Statement as a British Hans Christian Andersen Ambassador

Fairy tales hold an attraction partly because of their universality; they have been around in various forms and cultures for centuries. They reach into the core of nostalgia for childhood; they offer comfort. What is thus compelling for some writers is the potentiality of these tales for subversion; the malleability of their structures; the opportunity to play with their conventions. In the late twentieth century, many writers – particularly female – reworked fairy stories. Angela Carter, for instance, eschewed the old rigid gender roles and female masochisms, reinventing these tales as more liberatory for women. I think A. S. Byatt too found freedom on entering into territories other than conventional realism, such as the past and the wonder tale, often mixed with domestic reality. The instability of the fairy tale and the identities within it open the door for self-conscious parody and irony, bringing freshness to an old genre. Previously passive princesses can change their destinies. The multi-genred *Possession: A Romance* (1990) marked a turning point in Byatt's career, helping her to discover her writer's identity, leading much of her future work (whether short story, novel or novella) to include overt or embedded magical

Writing A Tale

elements. There's freedom in wearing the cloak of the fairy tale.

A. S. Byatt reveals her concept of fairy tale images as a way of understanding the working of imagination: 'You can understand a lot about yourself by working out which fairytale you use to present your world to yourself in.'[1] This is a close examination of some of Byatt's own fairy tale texts, wherein can be discerned, overtly and covertly, manifestations of the writer and her struggles and desires.

TALE OF THE UNEXPECTED

First, 'The Story of The Eldest Princess' from *The Djinn in the Nightingale's Eye* (Chatto & Windus, 1994), which Byatt describes as the story of her own life because she has always worried about being the eldest sister.[2] This is a self-reflexive story with a metanarrative where the narrator constantly demonstrates self-awareness both as author and character that she is in a fairy tale with all its inherent expectations and adventures. Even the title of 'The Story of The Eldest Princess' draws attention to its status as a constructed story and Byatt inserts classic themes such as royalty, a quest, animal helpers, the old crone and a 'once upon a time' opening line. The story is of a kingdom where the blue sky has disappeared and been replaced by a green one, and there must be a Quest undertaken by the three princesses to find a silver bird and her nest in order to effect a cure for the unwarranted greenness.

The traditional roles of fairy princesses are rather limited in scope, with royal heroines usually passive and silent, awaiting a prince who can wake them, make them laugh or marry them after winning them as a prize. Jennifer Waelti-Walters says: 'In every really famous tale the heroine [for example, Rapunzel, Snow White, Sleeping Beauty, Cinderella] is systematically deprived of affection, stimulation, pleasurable activity, instruction and even companionship' resulting in a 'lifeless humanoid, malleable,

---

[1] A. S. Byatt & Ignês Sodré, ed. Rebecca Swift, *Imagining Characters: Six Conversations about Women Writers*, (Vintage, London, 1995), p74.
[2] A. S. Byatt, *The Djinn in the Nightingale's Eye* (Vintage, London, 1995), p280.

decorative, and interchangeable'.[3] So, how can a princess find autonomy and learn by her own experience? The self-reflexivity lies in the characters' knowledge of the framework in which they exist. They are compelled by an intrinsic fairy tale motif whose ideology interpellates them. For instance, the eldest princess has read stories about princes and princesses who set out on quests, and has noticed the narrative patterns that emerge such as the inevitable failure of the oldest who will possibly be turned to stone until the youngest comes to the rescue.

'I am in a pattern I know, and I suspect I have no power to break it', ponders the princess. Like Red Riding Hood, she mustn't deviate from the path, but her foreknowledge actually does arm her with the ability to deconstruct the story and extricate herself from its bounds. She meets injured creatures (a scorpion, toad and cockroach) upon her way and chooses to help them by leaving the road and entering the forest in order to find a wise old woman. The Toad knows he won't turn into a prince 'or any such nonsense', but if tales are nonsense then what is the status of these characters in a quasi-conventional story of princesses and talking creatures? I think they are ciphers used to reveal their own constructions. A Bluebeard-type appears in the form of the Woodcutter who doesn't actually kill his wives – they just lose the will to live; the Cockroach warns the princess and she listens. When the scorpion's and toad's stock stories don't come true (no tricksy stinging and no turning into a prince), she realizes 'I *could* just walk out of this inconvenient story and go my own way'. Once she sees an alternative route, she understands the restrictions and oppressions of the whole scenario.

Marina Warner's book *From the Beast to the Blonde* particularly relates to women's historical position within the framework of tale-telling. She writes about Charles Perrault's female contemporaries who used fairy tale to try and escape the limitations imposed on women's destinies: 'The fairy tale looks at the ogre like Bluebeard . . . in order to disenchant him.'[4] She also talks about the oral tradition and the construction of the Mother

---

[3] Jennifer Waelti-Walters, *Fairy Tales and the Female Imagination* (Eden Press Inc, Montreal, 1982), p2.
[4] Marina Warner, *From the Beast to the Blonde. On Fairy Tales and Their Tellers* (Vintage, London, 1995), p24.

Writing A Tale

Goose storyteller which demonizes the 'old crone' figure. She claims that 'the thrust towards universal significance has obscured the genre's equal powers to illuminate experiences embedded in social and material conditions,'[5] meaning that fairy tales should be considered in terms of their historical positioning because they and the way they are interpreted change diachronically. She says: 'no story is ever the same as its source or model, the chemistry of narrator and audience changes it.'[6] We need look no further than Jack Zipes's study of the historical transformations of 'Little Red Riding Hood', which demonstrates how an oral folktale from female sewing communities about the social ritual of initiation of a young girl into adulthood is altered 'into a tragic one of violence in which the girl is blamed for her own violation.'[7] In Byatt's story, the wise old woman (a 'Mother Goose' figure) says: 'You had the sense to see you were caught in a story, and the sense to see that you could change it into another one', and asks what's wrong with a green sky anyway? The role of storyteller within this tale is interesting. 'We have no story of our own here, we are free, as old women are free, who don't have to worry about princes or kingdoms' – the wise woman has the freedom to imagine, invent and change stories as she is outside the romantic requirements and jurisdiction of the worlds she describes. She uses tale-telling as a form of psychotherapy to heal bodies and minds, which also activates self-empowerment in the others. The princess and creatures all become 'Mother Goose' in turn as they give their stories, the princess delighting in the *telling* rather than in being the told.

Having rebelled against her designated role, the princess assumes the quest will continue without her – the entire framework will not break down just because she has altered the content and left the plot. However, she has disrupted the inevitable outcome – inviting possible variations. The second princess also outwits the confines of her story and leaves the youngest princess without a story. Each woman is shown to

---
5 Marina Warner, *From the Beast to the Blonde*, p xviii.
6 Ibid. p418.
7 Jack Zipes, *The Trials and Tribulations of Little Red Riding Hood*, (Routledge, New York/London, 1993), p7.

overturn her expected fate. The key to this fairy revolution lies in the power of the role of the teller:

> There is always an old woman ahead of you on a journey, and there is always an old woman behind you too, and they are not always the same, and may be fearful or kindly, dangerous or delightful, as the road shifts, and you speed along it.

If the road shifts, then the teller and the told shift too; if 'Mother Goose' is not the generic old crone but changes as it suits her, then the characters in her stories can change their destinies too.

BLOCKING OUT THE WORLD

> *'Ah, boiler-room . . . this is the place in this school that I most loved . . . This was my solitary space.'*[8]

Byatt was the despised clever child who sought her hated school's boiler-room as a place of respite where she could escape from others and write stories. In 'The Changeling', from *Sugar and Other Stories* (Chatto & Windus, 1987), Josephine is a writer whose stories centre on fearful boys; she has written a book called 'The Boiler-Room' about a persecuted boy called Simon Vowle. She also fosters 'Lost Boys', a literary allusion applied to these displaced children. It is more subtle for Josephine to write about boys, in order to veil the autobiographical aspects of her work. Her writing is a channel for her own fear and she feels threatened when the character of Simon Vowle has seemingly come to life in the form of a boy, the pale and ghost-like Henry Smee, who comes to stay at her home. So threatened, in fact, that she gets writer's block.

Josephine hides from domesticity, but draws on the strength gained in *having* to face it. She becomes a hybrid, a self-constructed housewife-and-mother *and* a writer. The former is a

---
8 *A. S. Byatt: A Curious Mind*, BBC 2, 30/03/1996.

Writing A Tale

rather successful pretence, but the latter is the 'real' her. She controls her home and manages her family, as well as the stray waifs who come to her; but they don't impinge upon her creative space and energy – unlike J M Barrie's Wendy who told stories to the boys, Josephine retains maternal power by secretly learning and reusing their stories in her work. Until, that is, the arrival of the unfathomable Henry Smee who represents the threat of one half of her world to the other. Indeed, he undertakes an intellectual battle to the death with his hostess.

Byatt uses the metaphor of enclosure to depict Josephine's separation of her diverse selves. Being enclosed may be claustrophobic but it *is* an escape into a space that she can re-create as 'home', making it *heimlich*, furnished with her own ideas. This space can then enable her to reach out into the world, which is how Josephine's writing emerges. But her problem is finding a balance between being out in the world while remaining shut off from it. How can she engage with readers via her books while maintaining a self that is somehow separate and unreadable? Josephine sees the opportunity for controlling, rather than being consumed by, the situation; she sees the benefits of using enclosure for her own gain, for widening the space into a place for expression and later re-lives the pleasures of the freedom of being able to hide. Why is separation from others, or into two separate selves, so essential for her successful literary expression? Josephine and Henry Smee are brought together to play out a competition on the mental plane, where the threat of Henry lies in his *fusion* with Josephine.

The rupture of Josephine's carefully structured dual worlds begins when Henry is described as resembling the fictional Simon. Josephine's 'The Boiler-Room' is a surreal story of a boy in a boarding school who builds himself 'a Crusoe-like burrow or retreat in the dust behind the coiling pipe-system of the coke-boiler in the school basement and finally moved in there completely, making forays for food and drink at night.' It is as if a 'whole' version of Simon has been rendered in flesh and blood, but Henry Smee is compromised; he can't actually *be* Simon but his Henryness is somewhat undermined. Most worrying for Josephine is that she starts to lose control of Simon's image and

Sarah Gooderson

she is irritated by the intrusion into her creation. Henry is thus depicted as a fraud, a real person who is trying to be a constructed character – a stealthy, changeling boy. For whom is he a substitute? Just Simon? All of Josephine's fictional boys? The nexus of her creativity? Or does Henry represent dissolution of the 'real' Josephine, an identity that she keeps in a discrete box that functions alongside, but in opposition to, the Josephine who exists in the domestic sphere?

The language used to describe Henry paints him as an almost intangible figure, as his presence is refracted through Josephine's interpretation of his image. 'He was excessively thin and pale, with lank, colourless hair, moon-glasses and a long fragile head on hunched shoulders, the sharp bones standing out on cheek and chin' with 'Simon Vowle paleness'. Once Henry has embodied fact and fiction, these become increasingly blurred for Josephine. Has she drawn Simon from the archetypal outsider, or is Simon the palette used for painting the Henry canvas? This is the climax of the merger. Henry has 'a habit of stasis', but he also moves about like a permeating fluid. This paradox of stillness and fragile movement creates a quandary for Josephine. On the one hand, he is a real boy who seems to have no will of his own and is malleable; she uses her mood to gauge his, she actively reads him as a passive text – she is the writer and he is the object. But on the other hand, he is slippery and moves into the realms of being an unreadable text beyond Josephine's interpretative domain, which produces fear in her.

This terror of losing control leads to an anguishing search for an inviolate space, combined with a feeling that this place cannot be found 'out in the world'. If one is 'not at home in the world' where else is there to go? Josephine disappears into the pleasure-giving activity of writing. Here, she deals with her fear by writing of the terror as being outside. Writing is the door which shuts her in and shuts the world out. This connection between fear, enclosed spaces and the creative imagination allows these elements to feed off each other. Being one of the 'lost, voiceless sufferers locked in cupboards' is a torment when inflicted by others, but a self-imposed exile into the boiler-room is a delight. The sanctuary that enables expression is a form of seclusion, a

Writing A Tale

framework into which Josephine thinks she has incorporated freedom, but a freedom where one keeps one's self to one's self. It's not just a fear of going into the world, but rather a fear of infiltration *by* the world.

Imagine the terror of someone trying to penetrate that world. For Josephine, her creativity is violated. She can't bear to be told about Henry by Henry – she has already written him in her own words and doesn't want a re-edit. The battle is for authorial ownership. If the creation of Simon is an exorcism, then Henry is the ghost come back to haunt her. She is losing control of fear – and that is the crux of the problem. What she has written to contain her fear has materialized – it has leapt off the page and into the world. Byatt has said that *Possession* contains 'a sort of passionate plea for readers to be allowed to identify with characters,'[9] but here Henry's identification with Simon is a form of theft, which violates the mode through which Josephine channels her excess – that's why she gets writer's block. New Critic Cleanth Brooks says of I A Richards that he 'has endeavoured to maintain a careful distinction between the emotional state produced in the reader . . . and the means used to produce this emotional state,'[10] but Byatt shows that permeation and identification are unavoidable.

On a superficial level, Josephine cannot engage with Henry and learn his 'inside', but on a deeper level they are utterly locked together. She sacrifices time and effort for the other boys, as women have historically looked after others, but Henry involves the sacrifice of something more crucial, and so one of them has to go. Henry leaves Josephine's house and literally withers away without her. Josephine begins to imagine him once he's dead. His identity becomes less specific, more blurred, more malleable. Her writer's block lifts. She can steal him back now and write him, sketch certain aspects, design chosen characteristics: 'her imagination tidied Henry Smee into a mnemonic, a barely specified bed, a barely specified bottle, a form with one outflung arm'. She regains control over herself, her identities and her art.

[9] Nicolas Tredell, 'A. S. Byatt in Conversation', *PN Review* (Volume 17, Number 3, Jan/Feb 1991), p25.
[10] W K Wimsatt & Cleanth Brooks, *Modern Criticism: A Short History* (Routledge & Kegan Paul, London, 1970), p623.

Sarah Gooderson

She imbibes Henry as if she has artistically consumed him by osmosis. In her new story, 'the ghost of those limp yet skilful hands, just that, attached itself to the form of the present Simon (whose name was in fact James) but not so that anyone would have noticed.'

LIFE GOT COLD

A. S. Byatt says of 'Cold' (in *Elementals: Stories of Fire and Ice*, Chatto & Windus, 1998) that it is a 'metaphor for the writer in myself', a story of an Ice Princess 'whose existence is predicated on not making contact.'[11] But 'not making contact' with what? Princess Fiammarosa is surrounded by the warm protection of her family, which makes it difficult for her to act upon her true icy desires. After secret frolicking in the snow, her body becomes encased in an extra skin of ice, which does not cloak her identity – because it *is* her identity. Her new mantle defines her difference from others, but how can this crackable outer boundary survive their attentions? When her preference for coldness is discovered by her tutor, 'her whiteness became whiter, the ice-skin thicker' – he understands her separateness and thus her self-enclosure becomes liberating. This is unsurprising when in contrast with her claustrophobic childhood: 'I felt constantly that I must collapse, vanish, fall into a faint, stifle'. She finds a breath of life in her newly-realized loneliness and experiences sensation in her new skin: 'There was more life in coldness. In solitude. Inside a crackling skin of protective ice that was also a sensuous delight'.

Fiammarosa becomes further separated from the rest of the kingdom when not only is she given her own icy section of the palace but she becomes less understood and loved. Yet, it is now that her creativity is unleashed, in the form of original striking tapestries expressed in 'ice-blue threads'. The preciousness of her artistry is paramount, born of a thriving existence predicated on not making contact. Her father is her enemy in this respect, as he wishes her 'to be softened and opened to the world . . . to be

---

[11] Byatt, A. S., in conversation at 'Visiting Writers' season, at the University of East Anglia, 15 Feb 2000.

Writing A Tale

melted smooth'; he wants the hermetic cold seal to be permeated and dissolved by conjugal union.

In this metaphorical tale, metaphor proves to begin the undoing of the Ice Princess because she is a very single-minded interpreter. Her suitor Prince Sasan's gifts are crafted from glass, shimmering metaphors that reflect his desire to capture her: a castle that mirrors his heart – 'a poetic image of his empty life'; a beehive that represents 'the summer world' evoked by thoughts of the Princess; and a tree that embodies all the seasons. The Princess's senses tingle only to the crystal clarity of the form and the texture of the cool glass; she is blind to the crafted rosy flames, the warm, gold quality of the honey, and the rich summer season. Her interpretation of glass as resembling frozen water leads her to marry Prince Sasan, even though she learns that glass has been created from desert sand in 'a furnace of flames'. After the heat of lovemaking with the warm Sasan, Fiammarosa begins to melt inside and her icy centre and boundaries start to dissolve. Once in Sasan's desert kingdom, she recognizes the passion of her sexuality in the heat of the glass-making process, so what represents danger in the external world is also inside her soul. Her surroundings weaken her bodily and mental power but she is revived by entering the manifest metaphor for the Prince's heart – a life-size palace he has constructed for her from glass on a snowy mountain, where her protective ice layer reappears and re-forms her fading identity. Fiammarosa makes a compromise with Sasan's creative imagination, and is enabled to recommence study and writing. Thus, I think 'Cold' presents 'making contact' as a positive creative process.

STONE ME

So, finding space for expression is paramount, whether devising a new strategy for survival, defeating encroachments upon one's creative drive or travelling to an ice kingdom. Reversal of expectation is a common trait in these Byatt stories; the rebellious princesses and the self-serving mother all find some sort of artistic liberation. What of 'A Stone Woman' (*Little Black*

Sarah Gooderson

Book of Stories, Chatto & Windus, 2003)? Here, a woman (who works as an etymologist) faces decay and death but finds surprising revitalization. There is a similarity with 'Cold', in that rather hazardous bodily change encourages creativity.

Ines is confronted with disintegration wherever she turns. Her mother dies and is cremated, leaving Ines numb with grief; there is no more love. There is also a distinct lack of colour; everything's pale and bland, right down to the food. The story appears to be realist – Ines becomes seriously ill with a twisted gut, but her operation and the drugs she has to take, as well as the threat of plastic surgery, point to that staple of wonder tales and myths viz. metamorphosis. The turning point comes with the paradoxes of pain and numbness that she experiences, and the 'life gone out of objects'. No longer able to fill time with action, she notices the loofah, sponge and pumice in her bath are 'solids with holes'. She notices absence as well as presence, the intricacies of inanimate objects that have an alternate life as plant, animal and molten lava. Her perception has thus changed, establishing a past and a present, and Ines slips in the gap between.

Ines's body changes, becoming gritty, glittering, and crusty – she realizes she's slowly changing into stone. Not the plain, grey, solid stone that is the fairy tale archetype, the motionless statue of myth that binds all flesh and feeling by spell, but a mosaic of beautiful, colourful, light-capturing tesserae. Colour – '*Glinting red dust*', '*from ochre to scarlet, from garnet to cinnabar*' – replaces colourlessness. There's the noise and movement. And words. Lots of arcane, etymologically challenging words. *Jagged flakes of silica and nodes of basalt, rubious spinels, milky quartz, bubbles of sinter, hornblende, omphacite, gneiss, tuff, geyserite and hydrophane, shimmer of labradorite, dikes of dolerites, ultramafic black rocks, azurmalachite.* Ines hears the crackling noises and her body perversely comes alive within its solidification; some of the stone is conversely hot and volcanic. Her senses become sharper and her arthritis disappears.

Like Gregor Samsa's transformation into an insect in Kafka's *Metamorphosis*, Ines's experience is *sui generis*, and she escapes her life while retaining her consciousness. Whereas Gregor's

Writing A Tale

predicament is very much reflected in the other characters' repugnance, who can not accept that the monstrosity is still him, Ines's changes are represented in her own eyes as a newfound beauty. Life in the mineral world is definitely not the end. She accepts her fate: 'I should stand outside for when I am solid'. This is no spell, no curse or punishment; it's not something from which Ines needs to be freed and returned to normality. She meets Thorsteinn, a stonecutter, telling him, ambiguously: 'I am interested in stone work. Maybe you can make me a monument.' She goes to his homeland, Iceland, with him and poses so that he can sculpt her. His regular stone statues are formless, blind stumps by comparison. Thorsteinn is an anti-Pygmalion in this modern myth; instead of sculpting a beautiful woman and wishing for her to come to life, he has a living woman from whose likeness he makes a sculpture while she is metamorphosing back into a base form. She is an organic beauty who becomes more real and solid while Thorsteinn and other things become lighter. Creatures take up home upon her rocky surface; she is a living monument, an organic work of art that changes and grows. Traditionally, trolls' dwelling places include mountains and, in Scandinavian fairy tales, trolls often turn to stone. In her new Scandinavian home, Ines ceases to be the static model and returns to the mountains, a troll woman who has found liberation in her stony state – 'You are a metamorphosis', Thorsteinn tells her.

At the centre of this story are transformation, creative freedom and wordiness. The discovery of new and unusual words – with their classical roots, scientific register, many colours and rich, vibrant textures – is as pleasurable as Ines finds the petrification.

*

So, 'The Story of the Eldest Princess' has a traditional fairy tale structure with a woman rewriting her way out; 'The Changeling' is a realist story with supernatural undertones where the writer is under threat; 'Cold', with its classic prince and princess, is the prevailing metaphor for the writer who craves the right

Sarah Gooderson

environment; and 'The Stone Woman' is a realist/surrealist story where there is rebirth into a world of texture, colour and words instead of disintegration. Jack Zipes, in his study of the history of the romantic fairy tale, says a distinguishing feature is the displaced hero who is homeless in an alienating world or the artistic hero whose creativity is threatened by confinement.[12] These twisty, rule-defying tales are alive with characters who remake their own worlds and realign power structures, optimistic with a sense of artistic liberation, and brimming over with Byatt's wordy energy.

---

12 Jack Zipes, *Breaking the Magic Spell: Radical Theories of Folk and Fairy Tales* (Heinemann Educational Books Ltd, London, 1979) p65.

simon@pform.co.uk

Dubravka Ugresic
Welcome!

A writer without a nation is like shit in the rain.
— Jonas Pshibiliauskiene-Krikshchiunas

Zeus, the father of all gods, is smiling benevolently as he watches his favourite Europa at work. She can't be said to have betrayed his expectations. He had none. When he left her, he gave her two gifts that any woman might covet: a spear that never missed its mark, and expensive jewellery. After she used her lover to get her quickly to geographically more favourable and appealing climes, and after her erotic fling with the horned beast to whom she bore her sons, Europa, satisfied and sated, married a local fellow, Asterion. Poor Asterion has nothing more on his CV than marriage to Zeus's mistress and the adoption of her three bastard boys. But she, with her natural talent to do equally well by gods, animals and men, and with a small but significant sum of capital left to allay any subsequent moral damage, continued to live a so-called full life. That first journey on Zeus's back had stirred in her a yen for geography, so she explored new lands and continents. Many of them she colonized, and then de-colonized. So it was that she augmented her wealth. She invented many things. She declared absolute copyright on democracy, humanism, art, literature and philosophy. She was aggressive, too; she waged wars and honed the art of annihilation. Several decades ago she committed the most vast and terrible crime in the history of mankind, murdering some six million of her Jews, which in no way prevented her from playing the role of moral arbiter whenever subsequently she chose to.

Welcome!

Today Europa, like a good and wise mistress, is uniting her lands, although she flatly failed a recent unification test. She who did nothing to prevent the dismemberment of Yugoslavia and subsequent war is now spitting out phrases such as 'post-national units' and 'post-national constellations'. She, who never so much as blinked an eye at the disappearance of the 'Yugoslavs' – this was an ethnically indifferent 'mixed' minority living in the former Yugoslavia that was actually larger in number than the more nationally conscious Slovenes – is now demanding that a rigorous respect for the rights of minorities be a key requisite for joining her ranks.

Perhaps precisely because of this, and who knows what else, one of the key ideological cornerstones of European unification today is – culture. Just as each little town in the former Communist countries used to have its 'Culture Centre', so the large map of European integration is criss-crossed by virtual and real 'culture centres'. No one seems to know what the word 'culture' really means. Culture can be all and nothing: a smoke screen; a tourist-instructional gift packet offering a smattering of history; folklore, a line or two of verse; culture can serve as an *identity help kit*; as a language for diplomatic communication among nations; as a shadowy realm for self-respect and mutual regard; as an unfettered space into which meaning can be inscribed and read. Culture may be understood as a way of life, *whether of Berbers or barbers* as Terry Eagleton with wit notes, as the progression of cultural history from Seneca to Seinfeld, as the opposite of barbarism, as a symbol of romanticists, as a form of manipulation and superiority, as a mere marketing product, or as a synonym for *national identity*. The word *culture* fits conveniently into the vocabulary of the administrative EU newspeak. Because in that vocabulary the most frequent words are also the shadiest, such as *fluidity, mobility, fusion* . . .

In this new European context, culture is meant to be traditional, national and cosmopolitan – all, of course, in reasonable measure and balanced proportions. Culture should promote local colour, yet remain open, and of course culture should open borders at the same time it reinforces stereotypes. Every tourist ends his or her visit to Holland by purchasing a little pair of wooden clogs, a

Dubravka Ugresic

small windmill and a tulip bulb, despite the fact that the tulip is of Turkish origin, and wooden clogs are footwear worn by peasant populations in all the muddy northern European countries, and there are windmills spinning in *Don Quixote*. All this will not shake the resolve of the visitor to bring something back from their trip that is genuinely *Dutch*. The souvenir vendors meet the customers halfway. They know full well that whoever tries to break the stereotypes market ends up bankrupt.

Culture, therefore, is a representation of something. And art is a representation of something. In that most pedestrian of conceptual fusions, culture is tied to the broadly understood notion of 'art'. As far as art is concerned, Europa in her rich cultural history came up with patronage, a fertile partnership of art and money, which gave birth to the 'golden age' and the European cultural canon. Europa further explored the joining of art and ideology, bringing us periods when, as Walter Benjamin put it, 'Fascism aestheticized politics' and when 'Communism politicized art'. Europa explored various aesthetic canons, artistic concepts and periods, she tested long periods of elitist high culture and then a time of 'mechanical reproduction' and then she tried stripping art of its aura, only to find herself at the end in a tangle of concepts, but also in a fierce, chaotic dynamic where a number of things mingle: democratization of art and the rule of the market, domination of a largely American mass culture and the consequent geopolitization of culture – all standing shoulder to shoulder with the remnants of traditional cultural concepts and their politicization. And in the middle of this morass Europa treats culture as her principal ideological adhesive in order to rearticulate and redefine herself.

At first glance, there would seem to be no cause for concern. A brief stroll around the internet will demonstrate that Europa is nicely networked today with hundreds of highways, roads and byways, hundreds of funds and foundations, umbrella organizations, NGO networks, cultural services and virtual offices, whose sole task is to enable cultural traffic to flow unhindered. Countless cultural managers, officers, culture lawyers and culture mediators are busily facilitating the traffic of culture and cultural co-operation. These people are salaried

Welcome!

Europe enthusiasts: they are nationalists, post-nationalists and internationalists; they are cosmopolitans and globalists, they are European and regional nationalists, they are spokespeople for European local colour and differences but also European unification, in a word, they are professionals with multiple identities, people with several heads on a single body. European current and future cultural life exists in this dynamic, in the rich network of united European cultural bureaucrats and the still unnetworked direct producers of culture.

Though literature has long since lost its primacy, relinquishing pre-eminence to the more attractive and representative media, its life is still dictated by these cultural regulations and requirements. The contemporary European writer, particularly the Eastie, is a product of this confused cultural dynamic. He, too, is one body with several heads, and he does what he can to position himself to keep up with the changes. He discreetly attempts to retain his traditional role as the 'soul of the people.' In Eastern European countries this function has long since been depoliticized, but it persists quietly, as a sinecure. The newly joining countries (with the exception, possibly, of Malta) have not yet succeeded in expunging their 'liberating' nationalism, so the writer as the 'soul of the people' still has some utility. The model, therefore, has not lost its appeal. For the 'soul' of one nation best communicates with the 'soul' of another nation, but it is much harder to communicate with a 'soul' that has no borders and no permanent address, isn't it? Under the old conditions, our Lithuanian or Slovenian writer, defending the autonomy of the 'literary arts', declined, in some cases, to represent his (Communist) people. Today he is prepared to assume that role again. Why? For his (post-Communist) people? Because he has changed his attitude toward literature? No. Because of the law of artistic supply and demand. Because the European literary marketplace cannot survive an inundation of fifty Lithuanian writers (just as the Lithuanian marketplace can't sustain more than two Dutch writers, for example), and so only one or two will be welcome. This select two will be the 'household names' of Lithuanian literature. Hence today's Eastie is a European oriented 'soul' who craves affirmation from the

Dubravka Ugresic

European market, and a 'globalistic soul' who would sell his European affirmation tomorrow for a more profitable Anglo-American reception. This emergence from the paradise of national literature, where a writer is always treated as a 'representative' and 'an artist with words,' implies a further nod to market democracy. Writers from Slovakia to Slovenia who have been surrounded until now by short-sighted colleagues with generous rear ends, are now being faced with the market. On that market they are going to be running headlong into David Beckham, among others, who recently was given a British Book Award, because a book, bearing his name, brought the book industry a pile of money. That is why our Estonian, if he is a market optimist, will have to figure into his literary life regular visits to the fitness club. Because the competition is fierce, unfair and traumatic. True, the European cultural bureaucracy, at least in this transitional period, is allowing for a delay before facing the brutal realities of the marketplace, which still holds literary-national identities in high regard and promotes their exchange. These bureaucrats take their cut for that, as any agent does. And the readers push their own agenda. They would like to catch up with things in a hurry and read a little something *Estonian.*

What about those who have no national identity? The 'Daltonists', the cosmopolitan jet set and the intellectual proletarians, what about the spokespeople for a European identity, a European *melting pot* that would erase state borders, national and ethnic divisions and would be legally regulated by handing people a European passport and the status of a European citizen? Those (and I count myself among them!) will have to wait. The only thing people like us can entrust our Utopian hope to is the movement of major capital, although this may sound like a paradox. In the future, instead of nation and state, the new 'identity maker' may be a powerful corporation, and in that case it could happen that the logic of money simply does away with state borders and identities. If this should happen, Serbia might be renamed 'Ikea', and its inhabitants might be Ikeans, while Slovenia might be renamed Siemens, and its inhabitants might be the Siemensites.

Life itself seems to be moving quietly in that direction. The

Welcome!

East will not be moving westward with the acceptance of ten new members, as every anxious West European chauvinist has feared, but instead the West is moving eastward. I know nothing of the avenues of major capital, but I do know that the Croatian coast has been sold off for a song, that the Bulgarian city of Varna is full of averagely solvent Dutch, Belgians and Germans, the ones who were slow on the ball buying apartments in Dubrovnik, Prague or Budapest, so now they are snapping up what's left. It is entirely possible that these small, numerous and invisible migrants, these smalltime owners of Croatian, Hungarian, Bulgarian and Romanian residential property will determine the future of Europe, even the future of European culture. Why not? If nothing else, they know that life in the freshly incorporated, and especially in the not yet incorporated, countries of Europe will be cheaper and more fun than life in the expensive West European urban ghettos. Aside from that, there is that damned 'identity' stuff for export: from the amusingly oversized Bulgarian kebab to the cosmic singing of Bulgarian women.

As far as the reception of new members is concerned, I am thrilled to contemplate the French struggling to get their mouths around Lithuanian names and the Germans polishing their Latvian. I am also delighted that the Lithuanians – who are always boasting of the fact that Vilnius is the geographic centre of Europe – will now have to tone down their enthusiasm for their own national charms as they enter the European Union. I am also pleased that as they enter the EU the Estonians will have to edit out those verbose passages in their tourist guides describing the cornflower as a purely Estonian blossom, flourishing on Estonian soil for a thousand years. As we know so well, national identity is a matter of lengthy, intelligent marketing. I will say it once again: the national symbol of Holland is the tulip, formerly a Turkish flower.

And what about literature? Will it come out of this interaction changed? It will. I assume that in the first phase, Slovakian, Lithuanian and Letonian writers will donate the occasional book to the existing heap of tomes on people who suffered under Communism. In Belgrade, as I write this, belated souvenir vendors are selling little busts of Tito (30 Euros a piece).

Dubravka Ugresic

'These are for the foreigners, they like to take something Communist home with them,' say the street sellers! There will be attempts to sell similar souvenirs, but they will quickly vanish. The topography that had been lost in literature will, I assume, return. In Croatian novels in the late nineteenth century and early twentieth, for instance (and much the same is true for the Czech, Hungarian and other literatures), intellectual heroes travelled back and forth to Vienna, Prague and Budapest, speaking in German or French, and their books were printed without any of the footnotes we see today, translating all foreign language references into Croatian. The topography has become richer. From the Eastie's thematic repertoire, the themes of exile, passports and visas are gradually vanishing, as is the division in the European world of 'ours' and 'theirs'. But from the perspective of the negligible number of Westies interested in the European East, that superior-imperial component is also on its way out. It would, of course, be interesting if European writers were to take a good look at one another and write something about this. But the enthusiasm around unification and the code of political correctness would not allow them to. And the market will give incentive to lighter, younger literary themes.

As far as a fair subdivision of literature is concerned, something writers of smaller European literatures are particularly sensitive about, we aren't holding our breath. Because literature, too, is vulnerable to geopolitics. There is great, imperial Literature (with a capital 'L') bedecked with the trappings of universal literary values. There is, therefore, Literature, and – women's literature. Until the day we get a men's literature, women's will languish in her native ghetto. Much the same applies to the smaller and larger European literatures. Of the smaller literatures there are expectations of local, regional and national colour, while the large literatures are expected to bear the burden of universalism. So it is that the longed-for right to a native, national or race identity for literature turns into a punishment, a nightmare.

In closing, Miroslav Krleža had things to say several decades ago that are now well worth revisiting on the subject of European literary enlargement and literary geopolitics:

Welcome!

'What does one solitary book mean in the world today, no matter how deserving it may be of publication? Less than a droplet of water in the Amazon River. Four hundred years ago when Erasmus published his book in two hundred copies, this was an event for the European elite from Cambridge and Paris to Florence, while today, among the hundred-odd book fairs where hundreds of thousands of new books appear, how can a single, lost, solitary book be noticed? Great masters, who turn books into lucrative merchandise, the sovereigns of the metropoli of literature and art, govern the literary marketplace, taste and aesthetic criteria, and without the thunder of their propaganda thousands and thousands of books would disappear into a totally nameless silence. I do not mean to suggest that literary successes are manufactured by the press and advertisements, any more than fuss in the press can predict the winners of a horse race, but I hold it to be indisputable that a hypothetical reassessment of literary values today would give a different picture of the condition of the European book than the press of metropolitan centres does in its advertising. The structural value of the average or the whole of literary production would assume different proportions. Perhaps this would not essentially change today's criteria, but it certainly would multiply the gallery of loud names coming from those countries, which are cut off from the literary metropoli by the barrier of their unknown languages. At least cartographically the boundaries of good books would be broadened.'

Cecilia Rossi
Boilers

Suddenly the boilers started going. At first I didn't know what a boiler was, or that the very building where we lived also had one. But I thought it was all very stupid, to have these huge boilers located underground, even below the garage where the cars were parked, sometimes even as low as two floors below sea level, when they could explode, it seemed so easily, and send the whole building up in the sky like a hot air balloon. *What is a boiler?* I asked. They told me it was like a huge pot where hot water boiled day and night so that when we turned the tap on the ninth floor, the water would run warm and ready for us to shower or have a bath. And it was the same with the heating. The boiler was responsible for our warm floors, because there were pipes all over the place down there, *can you feel it here, right below the oak parquet*, like a complicated criss-cross of roads, so efficiently laid out that every corner of the house was warm in winter, in fact, sometimes really *boiling* hot, because although we do get a few cold winter days in Buenos Aires, it is not like, say, the cold winters they have in Europe . . . And it was the Romans, Mum said, who invented the system of underfloor heating. Then she walked towards the bookcase and chose the right volume of the *Children's Britannica*, to show me the pictures. And I saw Bath for the first time and the neat piles of bricks to hold the tiled floors and the fires underneath, kept by slaves whose skin glowed red in the heat . . . *But why do boilers explode?* This was really what worried me. Because if it was due to a fault in their structure, then ours could also go. Any time. The whole building, sent up in the air with the explosion, and my room too, my books and dolls and Mum and

Boilers

Dad and even my sisters, the whole of my life could just go in a matter of seconds and nothing would remain but ashes and burnt wood and flesh and wisps of hair, everything just growing cold slowly, and wet, under the firemen's hose, the way I'd seen it, only a few blocks from home, behind the fence they'd put up to keep people away.

I remember it was not very cold yet, perhaps winter was only just starting. And we were back to wearing the school uniform now after a few weeks when we were allowed to wear whatever we liked to school because we had to pretend we weren't going to school at all. It had to do with the kidnappings. And we knew that although we had slid back into our drab school tunics and white shirts and ties and blazers, if things started getting bad again, we would be sent home with a note asking please send your child in everyday clothes tomorrow, *not the school uniform*, until further notice. Somehow the uniform thing and the boilers were connected. I didn't understand entirely how, but knew that when I was woken up at night by the sound of an explosion and then kept awake by the sirens, a few days later we would be asked to leave our blazers and tunics at home.

And they happened quite regularly. Some were not very big, or loud – a minor fault, perhaps? I didn't dare ask. Did it mean that part of the building had gone up, and not the whole; floors one and two, say, and perhaps even bits of the third floor, but not beyond that point? I was secretly glad that this possibility existed, that we lived on the ninth floor, that somehow my neighbours on the first floor were more likely to get killed, their home dissolved in smoke and flames. And especially since the man on the first floor was a *Retired Military Man*, my dad said. He sounded serious. He sounded like he knew what he was on about, as if he had unravelled the whole mystery of the boilers and would be able to predict if there was a chance ours might ever go up or how big an explosion it'd cause if it ever did. Perhaps because he used to spend so much time down there, in the *baulera*, sorting out his 1940s car parts . . . But this man was nice, I wouldn't have wanted him killed . . . Who would walk his huge Dalmatian *Markus* if he went? They used to call him *el General*, I remember, but it was his wife who was the real *general*, there was no doubt

Cecilia Rossi

about it. She wouldn't let us play in the back patio, and it *was* a communal patio. We could all use it in theory, and just because their windows happened to open out on it didn't give them the right to complain that we were too loud or naughty or even horrible . . . We used to have fun, running around in the open patio when the weather was nice and we could enjoy the space that, after all, belonged to all of us. So we soon started calling her *la Generala* . . . only I think she never knew . . .

One Saturday I asked Dad to take me downstairs with him. I saw he had opened one of the kitchen cupboards, the largest, which he had completely taken over for his car parts, to Mum's dismay. She used to say her kitchen had been colonized, that it was no longer her own independent realm . . . I didn't quite know what she meant, to me the kitchen was big enough for everyone to have a cupboard and things stored in it. And we had three of the bottom ones, chock-full of toys. And it was nice and felt so safe when we could all sit there, my sisters and me, on the warm tiles by the open cupboards, a display of toys around us. Mum at the table with her sewing and Dad with his spare parts. All together under the same warm yellow pool of light of the kitchen lamp. Still, Dad's things seemed to irritate Mum more than anything else. As if on Saturday mornings, when she was planning the weekend's food and cooking, she especially needed to have all of her own private kitchen world to herself. And there was Dad, moving tiny box after small box after big box, *all 1940s original packaging* he'd got from this guy in Warnes, from the neatly arranged shelves inside the cupboard onto the kitchen table . . . He would soon go down, I knew, to fetch something larger, something like the front lights or the mudguard, or take a look at the spare 1947 *Dodge Sedan* door to see if it had moved in his absence, or fallen onto something else, or whatever his fancy would dictate. Me, I just wanted to get closer to the boiler . . .

In my mind the boiler had become this huge heart, pumping warm, thick blood to the whole building, to each and every room in every flat, and there were thirty-one in all . . . So we took the lift down to the garage, to the *subsuelo,* the 'under floor', though it sounded more like an *underworld* to me, where life existed as if in

Boilers

a parallel universe. Floor 01, this was as far down as the lift would go. Then we simply had to take the stairs, making sure we turned the light on first. It was pitch dark. And the smell tickled my nose immediately. It was *rat poison*, Dad said. Also, there was some powder sprayed in corners and against walls like a snail's trail, but dry and rather pinkish, to kill the cockroaches. They love it in there, Mum always said, because it is so warm. Because it was so close to the boiler. As we started down the stairs I could hear a strange soft purring, like the breathing of a huge animal. Then, once on floor 02, we turned right, to the *bauleras*. But I knew that I'd only have to turn left and I would see it: it was there, this immense hot cauldron of boiling liquid, this pumping centre of the building, of the world, of my entire world as I saw it then. And it was there, standing close to it, that I first felt the vertigo of the danger and fear I was soon to feel all the time outside when people discussed the killings and the bombs, when it was no longer boilers that went in the dead of night or accidental gas explosions in the city but real bombs and shootings even far north in provinces that I'd never visited but whose names I was made to learn by heart like rhyming poems in school . . .

But that was later, much later, after the revolution took place and the soldiers marched into town once more and once more the Plaza saw the tanks and heard the bombs and people had to leave work early and we were sent back home in the middle of the afternoon, like when Perón died. I remember that day. We were in English class and the mother of this friend of mine just came to the door and stood there and said she'd come to take her daughter home. Hadn't we all heard? *Perón is dead*. A strange silence followed then. It became really uncomfortable after a few seconds. Because then some more mothers arrived and picked their daughters up and no one was actually saying anything about what would happen to the rest of us, the *bus girls*. Eventually, we were all taken down and the buses finally arrived and everyone was trying to look casual like it was ordinary time-to-go-home time, only about an hour or so early. So by the time I got home, it was about four and it felt strange to be there. And early to have tea, although Mum also tried to look normal and put the kettle on and we had tea and buttered toast as usual, while we waited for Dad to come back from work. I sort of liked Perón. I liked him because he was on the telly a lot. Like every week, for a speech. And he'd raise his arms as if he was hugging the air and say *compañeros* in a way that made you think that the whole world was his special friend. I remember I'd said to Mum once, wasn't it a good thing that the president talked to the people so often. Mum was ironing. She looked at me, raised an eyebrow and said nothing. After a while she asked why did I think the president had to tell people things all the time, couldn't people decide for themselves? He wasn't supposed to be a father to us all . . . Dad couldn't stand him. He watched the news. The long queues to bid goodbye to the corpse. People wept and queued up all night and the flowers were incredible, only that we couldn't see the colours because television was still black and white then and colour TV was not to come for another four years, for the '78 World Cup . . . It was just like when Evita died, he said, and changed channels. Only to get another angle of the procession of mourners, another TV commentator, another shot of the dead man's face.

When Evita died, my dad said, the evening radio news changed times and instead of coming on at 8.30 they'd start at 8.25 and say *Eight-twenty-five, the hour when Evita entered immortality*. I didn't know what they would want to do that for but Dad said it was so that people didn't forget. *Forget what?* Forget how good she'd been, he said. It was Perón who didn't want to allow the people to forget, he explained, as she was so popular. I didn't see how Perón's second wife *Isabelita* would ever become that popular seeing she looked as ugly as she did. But anyway, there were many people out there who seemed to believe that Evita wasn't really dead and would indeed come back one day. It's true. I'd read it. There was this *Volveré y seré millones* graffiti scribbled all over Buenos Aires. I didn't quite understand how she could come back from the dead and be millions but it was there, on the walls, and it was always signed 'Evita' and sometimes 'JP' too, which I always thought stood for 'Juan Perón' but later learnt that it really meant *juventud peronista*. That'd been earlier in the year, I think, when Perón had got so angry at the young peronists, and at the *montoneros* too, and from the *Casa Rosada* he'd made a speech and all these people started shouting

Boilers

back and then walking away as they waved their blood red flags and the plaza soon became empty and there he was, an old man on the famous balcony talking to just a handful of people, older people of the 40s and 50s who were still loyal while the young ones had all marched away shouting revolution and muttering insults against old Perón, Isabelita and the rest of the gorillas . . .

And that was when the boilers started going. There was talk about how the soldiers would soon be called out into the streets, that the explosions had to cease, the kidnappings, the attacks on military bases . . . But I didn't quite understand how the soldiers could suddenly act as plumbers and sort out all the gas boilers around the city . . . And I was afraid to ask. Like I was afraid to see this man, the government's second or adviser to Isabelita, or whatever he was, but he was always there when she gave a speech and he even said once that the spirit of Perón ruled in him. Again, they were trying to keep him alive, I thought. Like with Evita . . . After all, they hadn't found the corpse, even when they'd killed this general who had supposedly said where she'd been buried, somewhere in the Vatican with the pope . . . *Aramburu*, I remember the name because it is Basque and my grandmother was Basque and her brothers too, all Basques who had fought a war and been sent to Argentina later, probably to recover because one of them had a stomach ulcer, Dad said because of too much drinking but at that point Mum always hushed him and said something about how in wars people eat very badly and sometimes they are even made to go without food for days on end and that's how he'd got that ulcer. Which is like a hole in the stomach, she said. I tried to imagine my Uncle Manuel walking around with a hole in the stomach but couldn't quite picture it because to me he looked quite normal, like he was in one piece. I never asked him anything about the war, because when people come back from war the last thing they want to do is talk about war, Mum always said, and she must have known that only too well and not just because of her Basque uncles but also because of her father who was Russian and had escaped a revolution and a war. Unlike my dad, who had lived through one revolution, he said, the '55 revolution against Perón and he was always talking

Cecilia Rossi

about it, about the bullets stuck in the government buildings around Plaza de Mayo, one day he'd show us, and blood on car seats, he'd seen it, all these beautiful 1940s cars destroyed, burnt down to their carcasses or made completely useless by the bullets, not even fit for getting spare parts out of them, such a waste . . .

I didn't know what was going on but it certainly felt like we were heading for war because food was sometimes scarce. Not that it was rationed and we got government cards or anything, like they did in Europe once, Mum had told me, but when we went to the supermarket we couldn't get as much of something as we wanted. Sugar, for example. And sometimes flour too. A kilo a person was the rule. It was scribbled in black on white paper and stuck at the entrance. So Mum would give us some money each, and tell us to go and get a kilo of flour and a kilo of sugar and then we had to queue up all on our own and pretend we didn't know each other so we could get away with it, get home with four kilos of sugar or flour or whatever it was. That was when all the kitchen cupboards needed to be used for storing food and Mum was really angry at Dad because he wouldn't take his car parts away and free up some space. Sometimes it felt as if they were fighting over all these little things, like where to store the sugar or the rice and what are you going to do with that front light, can't you take it downstairs, there's no more space, that's because you never throw anything away, not even the boxes, why would I want to throw these away, you know they are 1940s originals and imports, too, absolutely unobtainable now . . . Imports had been stopped and it felt as if people weren't travelling anymore and Thank God we managed a few days away by the sea in Mar del Plata that summer, where my grandfather had a little house. Only that Dad spent most of the time reading the papers and following the war in Tucumán, in the jungle, where the *guerrilleros* were fighting the soldiers and dying like flies and it was all going horribly wrong and my parents often talked to friends of theirs and Mum always said Thank God the girls are young, especially when she heard about this mother who'd been called in to identify her son and yes, she said, it's him, down there, at the bottom, as soon as she saw his hand-knitted socks, no need to see his face . . .

Boilers

And soon it was March and we had to start school again and we were back to wearing school uniform now and everything seemed to have gone back to normal. Even the boilers. Maybe the system had been changed and a more efficient way of heating water found. I don't know. I didn't dare to ask. Because things didn't get any better and the soldiers had been called out and there was talk of a *golpe*, which at first I thought meant someone had hit someone else but, no, it was my mistake, the soldiers had marched into town once more, Dad said. In school we traded stories. A friend had seen five, holding guns. And tanks, too. In my mind these soldiers became men holding brooms – perhaps something was said in the news, something about the need to sweep the house clean . . . I don't know . . . I only know that my fear of asking did not die that year and that for many years I used to hold my breath whenever I went down to the garage. And I never went down with Dad again to see where he stored his spare parts. Not even years later, when Mum said let's go down to the *baulera* and put some of these toys away, you never seem to want to play with them anymore . . . For me, this floor under the floor had indeed become a huge storage place where everything unwanted had been shoved away, brushed like under a carpet, all the questions I never asked had their answers buried down there, all the difficult words I didn't quite know what they meant, all the things I never dared name . . . who knows, perhaps a parallel world did exist somewhere underground, and this huge heart kept warm and alive by fear guarded me from it until I was old enough to understand.

Biographical Notes

Richard Beard is a graduate of the University of East Anglia's creative writing MA. He is the author of four novels: *X20* (Flamingo, 1996) is about a man who, every time he wants a cigarette, writes something down instead; *Damascus* (Flamingo, 1998) is a love-story set on a single day, 1 November 1993; *The Cartoonist* (Bloomsbury, 2000) is a novel set in and around Disneyland Paris; *Dry Bones* (Secker & Warburg, 2004) is a 'rollercoaster philosophical journey of Stoppard-like brilliance.' (Glasgow Herald). Richard Beard is also the author of a work of non-fiction, *Muddied Oafs, The Last Days of Rugger* (Yellow Jersey, 2003). He currently teaches at the University of Tokyo.

Ron Butlin's poetry and fiction have won many awards. Most recently, the French translation of his novel *The Sound of My Voice* gained the Prix MillePages 2004 and the Prix Lucioles 2005 (both for Best Foreign Novel). In 2004 he published *Vivaldi and the Number 3* (short stories), in 2005 *Without a Backward Glance: New and Selected Poems*. In 2006, *No More Angels* (short stories) and *Belonging* (novel) will appear. A regular contributor to the *Sunday Herald* and the *Times Literary Supplement*, he lives in Edinburgh with his wife, the writer Regi Claire. He is currently working on a new novel.

Biographical Notes

Simon Cass went to school in north Norfolk, and it is from his schooldays that a love of the coastline developed. The photographs are entirely digital and are almost exclusively of the coastline either in Norfolk or west Cornwall. Simon's work reflects the failed relationship between modern society and the land, which is increasingly seen as a leisure facility. His photographs are regularly shown in galleries around Norfolk, and are also available direct from <simon@pform.co.uk>.

Alison Croggon is a writer who lives in Melbourne, Australia. Her most recent poetry collections are *Attempts At Being* (Salt Publishing) and *The Common Flesh* (Arc Publications). Her young adult novels *The Gift* and *The Riddle* are published in the UK by Walker Books.

José Luis de Juan was born in Mallorca and studied Law and International Relations in Barcelona, Italy and the US. He is the award-winning author of five novels, a book of essays and a short story collection. His last publication, *Campos de Flandes*, combines photography with literary writing. His work has been translated to French, Italian, Russian and Turkish. Last year he took part in the prestigious Berlin Internationales Literatur Festival. Currently he lives at the Villa Waldberta in Munich where he was awarded a grant by the city to write his next novel.

Patricia Duncker is the author of three novels, *Hallucinating Foucault* (1996), *James Miranda Barry* (1999), *The Deadly Space Between* (2002), and two collections of short fiction, *Monsieur Shoushana's Lemon Trees* (1997) and *Seven Tales of Sex and Death* (2003), all of which have been widely translated. Her critical work includes *Sisters and Strangers: An Introduction to Contemporary Feminist Fiction* (Blackwell, 1992) and a collection of essays on writing and contemporary literature, *Writing on the Wall: Selected Essays* (Rivers Oram, 2002). Her next novel, *Miss Webster & Chérif* will be published by Bloomsbury in 2006. She is Professor of Creative Writing at the University of East Anglia.

Biographical Notes

Sarah Gooderson is currently studying part-time at the University of East Anglia for a PhD on the subject of A S Byatt, after receiving an MA there in Modern Literature, and a BA (Hons) in English & Film Studies from the University of North London. She has written and edited for Everyman's Millennium Project, freelanced as a copy-editor/proofreader, as well as worked for the Arts Council and for an independent television company.

Sebastian Groes studied English at the Free University, Amsterdam. In 2000, he emigrated to the United Kingdom, where he recently submitted his PhD on the representation of London in contemporary literature at the University of East Anglia. Besides working as an editor and critic for the Dutch-Flemish literary magazine *DW&B*, he published *McLiteratuur* (2004), a book on globalisation and literature. He has also published articles in peer-reviewed journals, an interview with Martin Amis, author profiles for the contemporary writers website of the British Council and edited a volume of essays on Ian McEwan.

Seamus Heaney lives in Dublin and teaches occasionally at Harvard University. A retrospective selection of his work is available in *Opened Ground, Selected Poems 1966-1996* and *Finders Keepers, Selected Prose 1971-2001*. His most recent publication was *The Burial at Thebes*, a translation of Sophocles' *Antigone*. A new book of poems, *Braird*, will be published by Faber in spring 2006.

Michael Holroyd has written, in addition to his biographies of Lytton Strachey, Augustus John and Bernard Shaw, two volumes of family memoirs, *Basil Street Blues* and *Mosaic*. He is currently President of the Royal Society of Literature and in 2005 won the David Cohen Prize for British Literature.

Selina Packard taught at Goldsmiths College, where she completed a PhD on fictional representations of Mary Shelley. Her abiding interest in and knowledge of Iberian language and culture motivated her to become a translator.

Biographical Notes

Pola Oloixárac teaches philosophy at the Universidad de Buenos Aires, where she is writing her thesis on Argentine Nationalism in the nineteen twenties and thirties. She has presented papers at the Congress of American Studies and the National Congress of Fantastic Literature. Her short story, *Acerca de la comunidad de hipotálamos y el código Morse*, was included in the *Anthology of Fantastic Literature* published in Argentina by Pagina 12. She is currently finishing her first novel.

Michèle Roberts is half-English and half-French. She has written twelve novels, two collections of poetry, three of short stories, one of essays, two plays and one film. *Daughters of the House* was shortlisted for the Booker Prize and won the W H Smith Literary Award (1993). Her most recent novel is *Reader, I Married Him* (2005). In 2002 she turned down an OBE. She is a Chevalier de l'Ordre des Arts et des Lettres and is Professor of Creative Writing at the University of East Anglia.

Cecilia Rossi was born in Buenos Aires and now lives in Norwich where she is completing a PhD in Literary Translation at the University of East Anglia. She holds an MA in Creative Writing from Cardiff University. Her poetry and translations have been published in various journals and magazines, including *New Welsh Review*, *Poetry Wales*, *Comparative Criticism* (CUP), *Point of Contact* (Syracuse University), *Modern Poetry in Translation*, as well as anthologized in *The Pterodactyl's Wing* (Parthian Books).

Martin Schifino was born in Buenos Aires in 1972. He studied comparative literature at the University of Buenos Aires and, in 1999, moved to London to do an MA in English at King's College. He regularly contributes to Argentine and English publications. He lives in London.

Biographical Notes

Errol Scott is a fiction writer, living in Munich. His work has appeared or is upcoming in several literary magazines in the UK, Canada, New Zealand, Turkey and the USA, including *Chapman, Cadenza, Connections* and *Lamport Court*. His work ranges across settings as diverse as the edge of the Gobi desert, the Japan Sea and coastal towns in America. Oceans and yachts, or the absence of desperately desired ships and water run through many of Errol Scott's recent stories. He is currently completing a collection of short stories.

Iain Sinclair was born in Cardiff in 1943. He has lived in (and written about) Hackney, East London, since 1969. His novels include *Downriver* (Winner of the James Tait Black Prize & the Encore Prize for the Year's Best Second Novel), *Radon Daughters, Landor's Tower* and, most recently, *Dining on Stones* (which was shortlisted for the Ondaatje Prize). Non-fiction books, exploring the myth and matter of London, include *Lights Out for the Territory* and *London Orbital*. In the 1990s, Iain Sinclair wrote and presented a number of films for BBC2's *Late Show* and has subsequently co-directed with Chris Petit four documentaries for Channel 4, one of which, *Asylum*, won the short film prize at the Montreal Festival.

David Solway's most recent book of poetry is *The Pallikari of Nesmine Rifat* (Goose Lane Editions, 2005). His previous volume, *Franklin's Passage* (McGill-Queen's University Press), was awarded Le Grand Prix du Livre de Montréal in 2004. His latest collection of literary criticism is *Director's Cut* (The Porcupine's Quill, 2003). Appointed poet-in-residence at Concordia University for 1999-2000, he is currently a contributing editor with Canadian Notes & Queries and an associate editor with Books in Canada.

Biographical Notes

Maxine Swann's short story, *Flower Children*, received the Cohen Award and was included in the Best American Short Stories, the Pushcart Prize collection and the O'Henry Prize Stories in 1998. Her first novel, *Serious Girls*, was published in 2003, and selected for the Booksense 76 List. She received a BA in Comparative Literature from Columbia University and a Master's degree in French Literature from the Université de Paris, La Sorbonne. Recent publications include articles in *Bookforum* and *Artforum* and stories in *Open City* and *Ploughshares*.

Dubravka Ugresic was born in former Yugoslavia (now Croatia). She is the author of several novels, short story collections and essays. Her books have been translated into almost all major European languages. Her books available in English translation are: *Ministry of Pain, Lend Me Your Character, Thank You For Not Reading, The Museum of Unconditional Surrender, The Culture of Lies, Have A Nice Day, In the Jaws of Life and Other Stories, Fording the Stream of Consciousness*. She has received several prestigious international literary awards. She is based in Amsterdam.

Luisa Valenzuela was born in Buenos Aires. She lived in the US from 1979-1989, where she taught at several universities. The shock of returning to Argentina is reflected in the short novel, *Realidad Nacional desde la Cama*, published in English as *Bedside Manners* (Serpent's Tail). Other books include the short story collections *Open Door, The Censors* and *Symmetries*, and the novels *Clara, He Who Searches, The Lizard's Tail*, and *Black Novel (with Argentines)*. *Strange Things Happen Here* (a collection of short stories and a novel) was exhibited in the *American Century* exhibition at the Whitney Museum, New York, 2000. Luisa Valenzuela's most recent books are *La Travesía* (a novel), *Peligrosas Palabras* (essays) and *Escritura y Secreto* (essays) and *Los deseos oscuros y los otros* (The New York diaries). She is currently working on a new novel, *El Mañana*.

Reactions

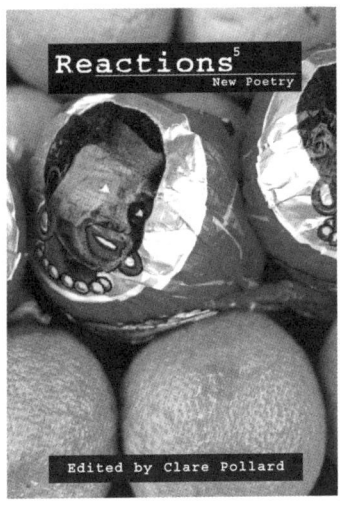

VOLUME 5
EDITED BY CLARE POLLARD

Reactions[5] is a showcase of exclusive work by the best new poets from the UK and abroad. It is a set of mini-collections all in one anthology, featuring poets who are at first collection stage or working towards it.

BUYING IS EASY . . .

For ONLY £7.99 (inc. p&p) per issue you get **Reactions** delivered direct to your door. Send a cheque payable to the **University of East Anglia**, to the address below. ISBN: 1-902913-24-8

REACTIONS • VOLUMES 1 – 4 • £7.99 EACH

Pen & Inc Press
School of Literature & Creative Writing, University of East Anglia
Norwich, Norfolk, NR4 7TJ, UK
info@penandinc.co.uk
+44(0)1603 592783

UEA NORWICH

www.inpressbooks.co.uk/penandinc

SUBMISSION GUIDELINES 2006

Pen & Inc Press is based at the University of East Anglia. It publishes a literary magazine, **Pretext**, which includes poetry, fiction, non-fiction and criticism; and **Reactions**, a poetry anthology for poets at first collection stage.

PRETEXT SUBMISSION GUIDELINES

Published twice a year, **Pretext** is a magazine of debate and criticism and, most importantly, a magazine of the imagination. **Pretext 12**'s general theme is: **India**. The deadline for submissions is 31 October 2005.

We publish an eclectic mix of fiction, prose, interview and poetry.

- Please submit all work typed in a plain legible font and double-spaced with address printed on each page. Cover letter or a brief intro is fine.

- The payment is £50 for accepted publication in **Pretext**.

- Submissions should be made by post only. **Faxes and emails are not accepted.** Please don't send computer disks.

- Please let us know if your work is being published elsewhere during this time.

- We do not send out acknowledgement letters.

- Timing: we aim to respond in five months. However, due to the volume of work to be considered, we have regularly exceeded this time span so be prepared for a potentially long wait. We do respond to every manuscript eventually.

- Enclose a Stamped Addressed Envelope or an International Reply Coupon if you are outside the UK. Please indicate (and enclose sufficient postage) if you would like your work returned.

- Submissions for **Pretext** should be sent to: Katri Skala, Pretext, Pen & Inc Press, School of Literature and Creative Writing, University of East Anglia, Norwich, Norfolk NR4 7TJ, UK.

www.inpressbooks.co.uk/penandinc

REACTIONS SUBMISSION GUIDELINES

Published annually, submissions are invited from writers who have had a first collection or pamphlet published (but not a second) and from those who have not yet reached that stage. The focus is on new talent.

- Submissions must be your own original work. It can be on any subject, in any style and of any length.

- Minimum of three poems, maximum of ten poems.

- Submissions should be written in English, but can be translations.

- Please submit all work typed in a plain legible font and with address printed on each page.

- Any submission must be accompanied by a covering letter that lists the titles of your poems, plus a short biography of no more than 70 words.

- The payment is £50 for accepted publication in **Reactions**.

- Your submission must not have been accepted for publication in any magazine (although poems due to appear in a first collection or anthology will be considered.)

- Please let us know if your work is being published elsewhere during this time.

- Submissions should be made by post only. **Faxes and emails are not accepted.** Please don't send computer disks.

- We do not send out acknowledgement letters.

- Timing: we aim to respond in six months. However, due to the volume of work to be considered, we have regularly exceeded this time span, so be prepared for a potentially long wait. We do respond to every manuscript eventually.

- Enclose a Stamped Addressed Envelope or an International Reply Coupon if you are outside the UK. Please indicate (and enclose sufficient postage) if you would like your work returned.

- Submissions for **Reactions** should be sent to: Clare Pollard, Editor, Pen & Inc Press, School of Literature and Creative Writing, University of East Anglia, Norwich, Norfolk NR4 7TJ, UK.

DEADLINE FOR SUBMISSIONS TO *REACTIONS* 6 IS 30 SEPTEMBER 2005
DEADLINE FOR SUBMISSIONS TO *REACTIONS* 7 IS 30 SEPTEMBER 2006

THE REAL READER'S QUARTERLY

Slightly Foxed

Do you carry elderly Penguins in your pockets?
Do you fondle fine bindings?
Do books furnish your room?

If so, we think you will enjoy *Slightly Foxed*, the lively and elegant quarterly that unearths books of lasting interest, old and new. Each issue contains 96 pages of personal recommendations from contributors who write with passion and wit. Eclectic and entertaining, *Slightly Foxed* aims to strike a blow for lasting quality – for the small and individual against the corporate and mass-produced. Why not join us, and enjoy some excellent company too?

'Absolutely beautifully produced',
JAMES NAUGHTIE, BBC Radio 4, *Today*

'Sparky and independent' *The Times*

'Packed with anecdotes, reminiscences and essays about books, writers and the trade. If you love books, you'll love *Slightly Foxed*' *Time Out*

'Brilliant . . . a great present for those who love books and live abroad' *Financial Times*

Annual subscription (4 issues of 96pp each) UK £32; single issue £8

Slightly Foxed, 67 Dickinson Court, 15 Brewhouse Yard, London ECIV 4JX
020 7549 2121/2111   all@foxedquarterly.com   www.foxedquarterly.com

NEW WRITING TYPES 2005

The New Writing Partnership presents **New Writing Types**, the second annual gathering for emerging writers with a serious commitment to their craft. Take part in writing workshops and meet invited publishing professionals and established authors in a series of lively panel debates and events.

The Writing Lab

Intensive workshops run by writers in residence in fiction, literary non-fiction and poetry. For serious new writers who are keen to examine their craft and creative processes. Tutors include: Joolz Denby, Kathryn Heyman, Tobias Hill, Romesh Gunesekera, Aminatta Forna, William Fiennes, Katrina Porteous and John Siddique.

Forum Panels

A series of discussions on the writing trade and issues of relevance to budding writers – every afternoon at 2pm, £7.

Writers in Focus

Everyday at 4.30-7pm. Distinguished writers provide an insight into their major influences and creative processes, from £7. Writers include Robert Macfarlane, James Meek, Michèle Roberts, Gervase Phinn and Kathleen Jamie.

One-off Workshops

Workshops with leading authors, including William Fiennes, Tobias Hill and Justine Picardie. Everyday at 4.30pm, from £10.

New Writing Types Live

Entertaining readings each evening at 8pm. Including Roger McGough, Saying and Doing. The Assembly House, Norwich, 8pm. Tickets £7.

Store-y-line

22–30 October at Jarrold the Store, Norwich. Free, lively literary events for all the family. Funded by Arts & Business.

One to One

Send 2000 words by October 1 2005 and book in for an individual session with one of our literary professionals. From £20.

For tickets and more information
call **NWP**, 01603 877177 or see www.newwritingpartnership.org.uk

The British Centre for Literary Translation

Translation today is situated at the very heart of literary writing. As this new volume of *Pretext* shows, English literature is written and read by people who share different linguistic and cultural backgrounds, a shuttling that finds expression in their writing, original or in translation. If you want to know more about literature in translation, why not sign up for the mailing list of the British Centre for Literary Translation by emailing bclt@uea.ac.uk? You can also check our website www.literarytranslation.com, run in partnership with The British Council Film & Literature Department.

Some of the events coming soon to BCLT

The 2005 Sebald Lecture

Given by Professor Germaine Greer, 'On not knowing (Aeolian) Greek: the metamorphoses of Sappho' at the UCL Bloomsbury, Gordon Street, London WC1H 0AH

7.30pm, Monday 3 October 2005
Tickets: £10 (£7 concs)
Box Office: 020 7388 8822
or book online at www.thebloomsbury.com

Dubravka Ugresic

Wednesday 12 October – 7.30pm
Drama Studio, University of East Anglia, Norwich

Organised in association with the Writers in Translation committee of English PEN and supported by Bloomberg (www.englishpen.org)

If you missed out on the opportunity to hear Dubravska Ugresic at our A Sense of Place events in June, here is your second chance. She will be reading from and discussing her new novel *The Ministry of Pain*, and we hope the translator Michael Heim will also be present.

InOtherWords

Issue 25: 'Self-translation' is now available. Submissions are also welcome for Issue 26 which explores the relationship between writer and translator.

From as little as £15 for two issues, a subscription to **InOtherWords** is excellent value so if you don't yet subscribe and would like to do so please get in touch:

**The British Centre for Literary Translation
School of Literature and Creative Writing
University of East Anglia, Norwich, NR4 7TJ.
Tel: 01603 592785 • Fax: 01603 592737
bclt@uea.ac.uk
http://www.uea.ac.uk**

Achintyarup Ray

BCLT is pleased to welcome Achintyarup Ray who will be joining us for three months this autumn as the 2005 Charles Wallace India Trust Translation Fellow. During this time he will be translating *The Hungry Tide* by Amitav Ghosh into Bengali as well as participating in seminars and workshops at UEA.

2006 and beyond . . .

In March we will once again be taking part in the Essex Book Festival where the focus of our events this year will be contemporary Dutch literature in translation, BCLT is also hosting a reading as part of a UK tour of international crime fiction writers including authors from Cuba, Finland and France (5 April tbc).

And although it's only a couple of months since the end of another successful BCLT Summer School, it's not too soon to put the date in your diary for next year. The 2006 Literary Translation Summer School will take place on 2-8 July at UEA, Norwich.

simon@pform.co.uk